Secrets from a Creativity Coach

Secrets from a Creativity Coach

Romney Oualline Nesbitt

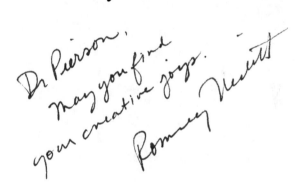

Buoy Up
Press

Denton Texas

Buoy Up Press
An imprint of AWOC.COM Publishing
P.O. Box 2819
Denton, TX 76202

Manufactured in the United States of America

ISBN: 978-0-937660-46-1

For my husband, Stoner, my faithful encourager.

Table of Contents

Introduction

My son stood in front of the open refrigerator—staring. "What did you do today?"

"I had a creativity coaching appointment," I said absently while I read the comics at the table.

"Were you able to help?"

"Um hum."

Cool air still escaping, he pulled out a carton of orange-mango juice and chugged it like a fraternity boy with beer. After swallowing he turned in my direction, "Give me the short version."

"Both/and instead of either/or."

"That easy, huh?"

"Sometimes."

That son is the college graduate, the one who paints, acts, and writes. Since he came home he's been washing dishes at a pricey downtown bar and restaurant. On breaks he performs his original spoken word poetry. He can't make up his mind what he wants to do. I'm sure he'll figure it out once he settles in L.A.

My younger son, wise beyond his years, is the one who decided he wanted to be a professional musician the day he placed a viola under his chin in middle school. He gets up everyday knowing exactly what he needs to do to create the life he wants to live, and he does it, day in, day out. We should all seek such clarity.

Both of these young men are determined to forge a life in the arts. These days when they call home they need more coaching than mothering. After a little polite chit-chat, I know the conversation will down-shift to a "how-to" question. We discuss decision making skills, time management, goal setting, contests, auditions, how to deal with the professional "gate keepers," and, of course, putting money in their ever-shrinking checking accounts. My sons are learning general life skills. They have some of the same kind of problems my creativity coaching clients bring to a session.

When I coach, my goal is to get to ask what I like to call "the next right question" and if we're all paying attention, the lost answer gets found. Sometimes, it's just that easy.

I do creativity coaching with schoolteachers, community theatre actors, church musicians, artists, writers and entrepreneurs. I teach classes on creativity to community college students. My clients and students take care of their families, volunteer in their community and still have the desire to build lives they really want to live. I try to help.

Through time in the classroom and in coffee shops talking one-on-one to clients, I've discovered some creative secrets I think will help you weave your favorite creative pursuit into your already busy lifestyle. You may want to paint, quilt, garden, be a stand-up comic, or write the great American novel. My goal is to give you my best creativity coaching tips in hopes that you'll find simple, practical solutions to the common challenges of the creative life.

You can coach yourself into a more productive lifestyle. You're uniquely qualified to be your own coach, agent and manager. It's your life and it's up to you to claim your creative goals and act on them. Let me show you the way.

I'll share a right-brain way to kick your habit of wasting time. My right-brain suggestions work for school age kids and PhDs. Did you know you can think an idea to death? Overanalyzing kills creativity! Procrastination and perfectionism can be conquered in six steps. Discover how ideas jump like leap frogs. Living in "someday" gets you nowhere fast and, "both/and" beats "either/or," any day of the week.

Breaking free from whatever it is that's keeping you from doing whatever you need to be doing, is worth your time, but I don't want to take too much of your time. Read this book like a road map. Take only enough information to get from where you are to where you want to be. The next time you feel lost or off-track, pull the map out again.

I've designed the book to allow you to tackle one problem at a time. Each chapter presents one tip or success strategy. Find your pet problem, try the solution, and get on with your day.

If you'd rather saturate your mind with self-coaching know-how, start on page one and go straight to the end, but don't use this book as another excuse for not living the life you say you want. Reading about doing your creative work or talking about doing your work is not the same as doing your work. Being able to do your creative work in the middle of a regular day is the whole goal of creativity coaching.

Coaching yourself takes honesty and willingness to spend some time thinking critically about your life. Some people find it best to ease into the process of change by reading about other people's problems and solutions. That's why I offer real life examples. Read the stories (with names and specifics changed), try the strategies and see if your life doesn't begin to have fewer creative interruptions.

A word of encouragement before we start: Creativity coaching is a process of asking the real questions, listening for the right answers and making the necessary changes. Simplistic, not easy, but always worth the effort.

Let's get started.

Romney Nesbitt

PART I:
Clarity for Creative People

Making a Life in the Arts

Michelle was a late-thirties, newly divorced, high school English teacher. She enrolled in my evening creativity class at the community college. Dressed professionally in a dark blazer she looked tired when she came into the first class a few minutes late. With an apologetically shy smile she slipped into an empty seat.

Michelle was part of our group, a dozen or so creative individuals, each with a dream of building a new life in the midst of their "regular" everyday life.

The class, "Self-Promotion for the Creative Person," included photographers, crafters, one musician, two actors, a motivational speaker, personal trainer and a couple of writers.

Class members introduced themselves and stated hopes for their present or future businesses. In addition to basic information, many took the opportunity to share honestly about their fears, frustrations and failures in past attempts to launch a business. This particular class was an especially generous group of caring people who were willing to share ideas and lessons learned from life experience.

When it was Michelle's turn to introduce herself she said, "Right now I'm a teacher but I want to be a writer."

Our chatty crafter who painted old prairie homestead scenes on saws blurted, "What do you want to write about?"

"I want to write a book about quilts," she stopped for a moment and then continued, "I want to promote the book by speaking to groups about quilts." She took another breath, "Wait a minute. I really want more than that." Michelle cleared her throat and in a loud, clear voice she announced, "I want to create and perform a one-woman show about quilts and the women who made them."

The class broke out into spontaneous applause. Michelle smiled as if she enjoyed the affirmation. We were all impressed. She'd clearly articulated exactly what she wanted to do.

"Wow, Michelle," I said, "You must have quite a passion for quilts. Tell us more."

"Quilts tell stories. There are stories about quilt patterns and stories about the women who made the quilts. I want to tell those stories."

"That's really an interesting idea. Have you been thinking about this for a long time?" I asked.

"I've loved quilts since my great grandmother used to make me a pallet on the floor. She would stack those beautiful handmade quilts three or four inches high to make a soft place for me to sleep. I felt so loved when she would tuck me in on that pallet." That thought made her smile.

"I remember sleeping on a pallet at my grandmother's house too," said the wedding photographer.

Michelle continued, "For some reason the night my divorce was final I had a dream about visiting my grandmother's house and sleeping on those handmade quilts." She looked down, "Ending a relationship makes a person think about all kinds of strange things." A few people nodded. Michelle looked around the room at the class, "I don't even really know why I signed up for this class. I guess I wanted to think about something different for a while. I don't really think I have the personality to be a performer."

"If you've been teaching high school then you're already a performer," I said. "Teachers play to the toughest audiences in the world!"

Michelle chuckled, "Well, you're right about that."

A writer in our group changed the subject, "Have you started your book on quilts?"

"Oh, no, I'm too busy. I teach high school. I tutor after school and grade papers in the evenings. My evenings are full. There doesn't seem to be any time to do anything I want to do right now."

"Have you thought about retiring from teaching?" a fellow student asked.

"No, I only have fifteen years left, then I can retire."

"Fifteen years?!" Once again, the crafter said what was on her mind and ours.

"I can wait," she said with a little bit of conviction. I wondered if she could.

"But, honestly," her body language suggested she was about to share a deep, dark secret, "I'm tired of giving. I need some time to myself to rethink the rest of my life. I'm looking forward to the summer break. I need some time to regroup."

"There's an African saying about slowing down to let your soul catch up with you. Does that phrase fit you and your circumstances?" I asked.

"Yes, slowing down is what I want to do and what I need to do. I'm hoping a summer off will renew my love for teaching."

"And if it doesn't?" the writer asked.

"Then I guess I'll look for something else to do," Michelle said.

"Like write your book?" another suggested hopefully.

"Or take an acting class to gain more confidence on the stage?" said the actor.

"Maybe." Michelle smiled. She dropped her head as a signal that I should move on to the next person. That was the last time Michelle spoke in class. In the next two classes she listened and took notes. In early August I received a phone call on a Wednesday afternoon.

"This is Michelle. I took a class from you last spring. I'm the English teacher. How soon could I meet with you?" She sounded anxious.

"Would tomorrow afternoon be soon enough?"

"Yes, that'll work. I've got an emergency on Friday."

This was something new. I've never been called for an "emergency" creativity coaching appointment. We made plans to meet at the regional library on Memorial Drive in Tulsa. I started to explain where we should meet, "The library has study rooms up…"

Michelle interrupted me. "I know where they are. I'll get there early."

The regional library in south Tulsa is one of my favorite places to meet with coaching clients. There are plenty of cozy corners for conversation as well as a coffee bar. On my way upstairs I picked up a latte.

At the top of the stairs I spotted Michelle. She stood guard in front of one of the study rooms. She was wearing jeans and a colorful blouse. She waved wildly as if to stop traffic.

"I've been here for fifteen minutes," she said breathlessly, "I couldn't move from this spot or we might lose the room."

I sat down at the tiny conference table in the study room. Michelle closed the door. I enjoyed a sip of my coffee and she pulled a bottle of water from her black leather bag.

"What's the emergency?" I asked.

"I think I want to quit my job."

"You want to resign from teaching?"

"Well, I'm not *sure* I want to quit, but I think I might. That's why I wanted to talk to you as soon as possible."

"Where's the fire?"

"I've got an interview tomorrow."

"For a different job?"

She nodded. Michelle's eyes brightened as she told me about the director's position at a small historical museum in western Oklahoma.

"Why is this appealing to you?"

"I did tell you I was interested in quilts, didn't I?"

"Yes, I remember." I had to scroll back in my memory to try to piece together the few words Michelle had spoken in class.

"My true interest is women's history and quilts," she was trying to help me make the connection.

"Is this a quilt museum?"

"No, it's just a historical museum. I guess there's a chance they might have quilts, but, women who quilt probably live in the area."

"Okay, I think I'm catching on. This little town could be a great place to do your research for your book on quilts."

"Absolutely!"

"Sounds perfect. So why'd you need to talk to me?"

"I'd have to quit teaching to take the job. This is the first of August. If I'm going to leave I have to give notice right away, this week!"

"That's right."

"Yes, but teaching is all I know."

"That's not true. You also know yourself. You said you wanted to write, publish, and perform."

"Yes, I did, but I wasn't planning on doing that any time soon."

"I remember you said you were planning on teaching for fifteen more years."

"That was the plan but once I said what I wanted out loud, the idea of doing something else wouldn't go away."

"It sometimes works that way. How'd you find this museum job?"

"The mother of a friend of mine lives in that town. She told her daughter the museum had posted the director's job. My friend thought I might be interested. I looked on the museum's website and my qualifications were not exactly a fit but close enough for me to send a resume. I never thought they would call me."

"But they did, and now you're going for an interview tomorrow."

"Romney, I looked up the town on a map. It's so small they probably don't even have a traffic light."

"And that means what?"

"Nothing to do!"

"Nothing except write, research, interview quilters and write your one-woman show."

She gasped. "Oh, my gosh. It's perfect."

"Could be. You know people who write books sometimes take a sabbatical at a retreat center for several months. They sequester themselves from the world to get their work done."

She clapped her hands in front of her face. She looked like a child in front of a birthday cake. "This job could be my sabbatical! I always wanted a sabbatical."

"And you can have one if you get the job. Every evening after work you go home and write."

"Home. That's another thing. The job has a house."

"You mean a parsonage, a manse? Like a minister gets?"

"Yes, the job includes a house to live in next door to the museum. That probably means the pay is really, really low." She frowned at that possibility.

"But living expenses would be lower than Tulsa too. No rent is a nice perk."

"Yeah, it is. I wonder what the house is like."

"I bet you'll find out tomorrow. After they meet you they'll probably take you next door to see it."

Michelle leaned across the table towards me. "What if they don't offer me the job?" Now she was worried she wouldn't get the job. She seemed to have forgotten all about teaching.

"Then you can go back to teaching. Nobody at school needs to know you went on an interview. You've got nothing to lose. It's a win/win either way."

For the rest of our hour Michelle talked about the relief she'd feel if she could get off the teaching merry-go-round. She shared her mixed feelings about making such a huge life change. I coached her to remember that every job is temporary. If she got the job and didn't like it she could always go back to teaching. After a while Michelle convinced herself she could be happy no matter how things played out the next day. She agreed to go to the interview with an open mind and as we parted she promised to let me know what happened. Two weeks later I received an envelope in the mail. The return address was a museum in Oklahoma. Inside the envelope was Michelle's new business card.

Michelle's new life just happened to be in a little museum in a quiet town with one traffic light on the western plains of Oklahoma.

I haven't heard from her since.

When Michelle claimed her dreams, she opened her heart to accept new ideas and possibilities. There's power in speaking your truth out loud, even if you don't have any idea how your dreams could come to pass.

A divorce and Michelle's quiet truthful awareness of her inability to keep on giving in the classroom were red flags.

Michelle slowed down and listened to her life. She admitted she didn't want to go through another year rushing to her job, taking work home, and falling into bed only to get up and do it again the next day. Times of focused and frenzied activity may be exhilarating for a while, but over an extended period of time they'll exhaust the body and soul.

Michelle knew she needed time to think, regroup and set a new course for her life, maybe that's why she took time away from grading papers to come to my three-night class on creativity. Like so many students in my classes, Michelle was finally willing to explore the new possibilities hidden in her talents, skills, and experience. She was ready to get back into the driver's seat of her life. She looked at a map of her life, charted a new course to her future and found the way home to her heart.

Make it Matter, Make it Happen

He had that trendy urban professional look. Narrow rectangular glasses framed his twenty-something face. He was thin, well dressed and quiet. Don was a student in my evening creativity coaching class at the local community college. I imagined he lived with his girlfriend in a cute mid-town Tulsa twenties-era home. He looked like the kind of guy who'd read Jerzy Kozinski novels in college and had an impressive collection of vintage comic books hidden in a closet.

Adults enrolled in non-credit classes are great students. When someone has worked all day in an office or hospital and then is willing to spend all evening seated in a hard plastic chair in an overly air-conditioned community college classroom, you know that person is looking for answers.

I wrote the assignment on the board: "Write your creative goal on a piece of paper. List three action steps to reach that goal."

Most of the students hesitated before they began writing. Don didn't waste any time. With one of those ergo-dynamic writing pens he scribbled off three quick lines on a white note card, sat back in his chair, crossed his arms and looked straight at me as if to say "Try this." The rest of the class members struggled with their lists for nearly five minutes. I really wanted to know what was on Don's paper.

"Anyone want to share their goals and action steps?"

Don raised his hand and I motioned to him. "I want to write a novel. The action steps are 1. Write the novel. 2. Sell it to a publisher. 3. Spend my royalty checks."

The class chuckled and nodded. We all enjoyed the zen simplicity of his appraisal of the writing process.

"Don," I said, "Would you be willing to participate in a little on-the-spot coaching?

"I'm game."

"Okay, let's analyze what you need to do to write your novel."

"Okay."

"Are you writing a novel now?"

18

"No."

"Short story?"

"No."

"Non-fiction?"

"No."

"Okay. You're thinking about writing?"

"Yes."

"If you were going to write a novel, short-story or something non-fiction, which would you choose to begin today?"

"A novel, I told you I wanted to write a novel."

"Yes, you did. Don, how long do you think it would take you to write a novel if you started today?" The speed of our conversational exchange slowed only for a moment while he did some quick mental calculations.

"Oh, probably two or three years."

"That's seems a little overwhelming. Would you consider a short story for starters?"

"Okay."

"A short story can be expanded to novel length or made into a screenplay. Short-short stories are 1500 words or so and novellas can be 20,000 words. What number sounds good to you?"

"10,000 words."

"Okay! Now we've got a word count goal. How soon would you like to have it finished?"

"Three months from today."

"What do you think you need to do first?"

"Write." He said this with the slightest hint of sarcasm.

"Exactly, but you said you don't write now."

"That's right, I don't."

"Why?"

"I don't have time." The students looked at me. All of them knew that saying you don't have time is an excuse that doesn't hold water in my coaching classes.

"What time do you get home from work?"

"About six."

"And then what do you do?"

"Eat dinner, clean up the kitchen."

"Then what?

"Watch TV or play a video game, or I do yard work if it needs it."

"Every night until you go to bed?"

"Yeah." The members of the class watched our conversational match, heads turning with each question and answer like spectators at Wimbledon.

"Do you ever think about writing while you're playing video games or mowing?"

"Yeah, I think about writing all the time."

"Does the urge ever hit you to stop what you're doing and go to your laptop instead?"

"Yeah, but I don't do it."

"Why not?" All eyes were on Don.

He paused and let out an exasperated breath before he spoke. "Because I don't have enough time to make any progress, so I do something that *shows,* like mowing. My girlfriend is happy when the yard looks nice. It's a no-brainer. The grass is high. I cut it. It looks good. My time and effort makes a difference."

All eyes were now on me. "Mowing makes sense," I said, "unless what you really want to do is write."

The classroom seemed especially quiet. Some looked down at their papers. "For most people, doing a job well is enough. Other people have bigger dreams. They want something extra. They want to accomplish something special. Don wants to write a novel. That's something *special.*"

The class looked in his direction and nodded approvingly. They were trying to encourage him but he wasn't ready to make eye contact. He uncrossed his arms and leaned forward very ready to listen now.

"Don, if you could figure out a way to write and see real results for your time and effort would that give you a good feeling?"

"Yeah, it might."

Don's excuse for not writing had nothing to do with time; he had plenty of free time. His reason for not writing was all about "mattering."

Don needed to feel as if his time counted for something—like it *mattered*. He wanted to see results for his efforts. A cut lawn was nice. It made him feel good to do the work. His girlfriend was happy, the neighbors were happy, but Don wasn't happy. He had simply found something to do that kept him busy that made him feel good. Not writing made him feel bad. He chose the good feeling over the bad feeling. Mowing was a noble substitute activity. Now all I had to do was help Don find a way to make writing feel good—maybe even better than mowing the lawn.

I stepped to the white board and wrote in all caps DOING WHAT MATTERS, MATTERS.

"Unless you do what really matters to *you,* you'll never feel any real satisfaction. Even if you do that *other* thing really, really well it won't feel like enough. Doing what matters is a way of making meaning in our lives. It's a way of creating a life that feels deep and full of purpose. Each of you must decide what matters to you."

I sat down on the edge of the table and faced the class. "You enrolled in this particular class because you have a creative dream. For some reason that made sense to you at the time, you pushed that dream aside, but you haven't forgotten what it is. In less than five minutes you were able to write your goal on a piece of paper and listed three action steps you must take to reach that goal."

I leaned forward and spoke softly, "You know what you want and you know how to get it. You don't need a mind reader. You only need to convince yourself that what you want to do matters enough to you to do it."

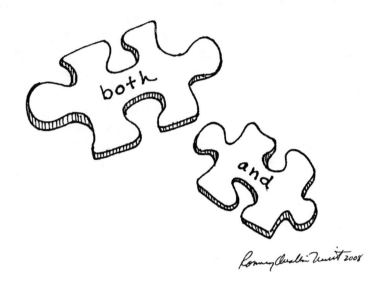

The Puzzle of "Both/And"

Jessica sent me an email:

Dear Romney,

I've been reading your coaching column in *Art Focus Oklahoma Magazine* for several months. I finally decided to stop analyzing and just make an appointment. I've taken up art making in mid-life and am a bit stalled out. My main job is managing my husband's landscape design company. I'd like to know how you do your creativity coaching sessions and what I can expect.

Sincerely,

Jessica Baxter

P.S. We used to work together at the library.

I replied.

Jessica, Yes, I remember. That was a long time ago. Glad you've found my column helpful. To find out more about my coaching, visit my website. When we meet, the first fifteen minutes are yours to ask any questions you have about my credentials, experience etc. The next hour is yours too. Tomorrow at 3 p.m. at Border's Books on 21st Street?

Romney

◆ ◆ ◆

We met in the bookstore café and settled into two nice leather chairs in the corner. After a couple of minutes of getting reacquainted she had a few questions about my coaching but she really wanted to know about my artwork, "So, tell me, are you still painting?"

"Yes, my most recent series was twelve watercolor portraits of women who represent female archetypes, you know, mother, maiden, crone plus nine more."

She seemed interested. "Where did that idea come from?"

"In seminary I was introduced to The Divine Feminine, you know Sophia?" She nodded so I continued, "Sophia put me on a trail to ancient goddesses, goddesses leapfrogged to Mary. Mary as 'Mother' reminded me of female archetypes. Of course, I went to the library and nosed around in the women's lit area until I found a book on female archetypes. Each archetype reminded me of a woman I knew."

"I wrote the names of those women in the margins," I whispered, "very faintly in pencil." She chuckled. Library people are particular about marks in books. "Don't worry. I erased the names before I returned the book." She laughed. "Start to finish, the series took about a year."

I checked to see if her body language told me she was sure that I did, in fact, practice what I preach as a creativity coach. Nestled back in the big leather chair with her coffee warming both hands she seemed satisfied with my answer.

"What would you like to talk about?" I asked.

She sat up and scooted to the edge of the chair, planted her feet and looked around. The café was still not very crowded. The semi-private space we had claimed was still ours. Jessica told me about her life.

She'd taken up painting a few years ago and preferred watercolors. Her kids were grown. Her part-time job was to manage her husband's business. She answered the phone, made appointments, greeted people, took care of the emails and kept the waiting room straightened.

"I have more time to call my own than I've ever had before, but I'm still not getting any art work done."

"Do you feel cramped by the time you spend at your husband's office?" I asked.

"No, not really. It helps us financially in that he doesn't have to hire someone to do the little stuff. It's fine. I probably just need to use my time in the evenings better."

"Most of us could do a better job of managing our time."

"I do especially enjoy part of what I do at the office."

My interest perked. "What part is that?"

"While I'm at the office I make little 'centerpieces' for the waiting room."

"Centerpieces?"

"Yeah, there's a square table in front of the couch. I covered it with cloth. I make arrangements of seashells or seeds, natural stuff with a candle in the middle. Some people don't realize it's special. They put their drinks on the cloth! So I made a big production out of putting coasters on the end tables to keep their cans off my centerpiece."

"How often do you make these centerpieces?"

"Not often enough for some people," she laughed, "some of the clients expect a new one every time they come in!"

"So you do a couple a month?"

She nodded. "People have been telling me I should take photographs of them or write a book about creating them—do something besides build one, tear it down, and build another one."

"Are you interesting in writing?" She shook her head. "Want to take photographs?" Another shake. "Tell me, what do you think your centerpieces do for people?"

"It's a visual resting space, you know a place to focus and calm down."

"By building these centerpieces, it sounds like you're making a real contribution to the work your husband does. You set the stage for something special to happen during their appointment. The centerpiece holds the space."

"Holds the space?"

"That's a spiritual direction term. My spiritual director always had a little arrangement of cloth and a cross and candle in her office when I would go in for my appointment. She said it held the space for the Divine."

She thinks about this for a minute. "I can see that."

The late afternoon crowd was coming in the café. A lady sat down in one of the nearby cushy chairs leaving only one empty chair as a buffer zone, too close now for where the conversation was going. I said, "Let's walk and talk."

We picked up our purses and coffees. I led us past the elevator to the winding staircase. Upstairs at Border's has a different feel. It's a quieter area full of books on world religion, metaphysics as well as CDs. The chairs on this level are Shaker style, serviceable and serious. We chose two overlooking the stairwell by a sale display.

I changed the subject. "Tell me how long it takes you to do the office chores each day."

She thought for a moment, "A couple of hours off and on in between appointments."

"And you're there for how long every day?"

"Four or five hours."

"Once you get people settled and they go in to the office how much time do you have?"

"Forty minutes or so."

"What do you do then?"

"I read some. Some days I make the centerpieces but that's only every once in a while. My daughter suggested I take my drawing table to the office."

Bingo.

"Sounds like you've got some time on your hands to do some art if you want, in between your work, you could paint."

"But I don't know what to paint."

She doesn't know what to paint? This is the moment I live for. I wait carefully, as I thought of the best way to phrase the obvious.

"The way you described your centerpiece reminds me of a still life."

"Oh!" She threw her hands up in the air as if she had walked into a hold-up. "I don't draw well enough to do a still life. Perspective? My skills aren't good enough to paint one of my centerpieces."

I shifted roles from coach to art teacher. "You could simplify the composition by drawing a birds-eye view of the still life, looking down. No perspective problems."

Her eyebrows went up in a hopeful slant.

I continued, "Something small, maybe 8 x 8" or 12 x 12"? Doable in short amounts of time?" I said this with a lilt at the end of my sentence. I was trying to create an opening for her to walk through.

"That does sound easier." She nodded her head, ever so slightly, and then looked up and to the right. I hoped she was visualizing herself at her drawing table in the office waiting room, happily painting the still life she had created both for the benefit of her husband's clients and for herself. Both/and.

Have you ever worked one of those two-sided jigsaw puzzles? The puzzle has pictures on the front and back sides, maybe a New England fall landscape on one side and a man in a hot air balloon on the other side. When all the pieces from one side are in place, a different picture appears on side two. Both/and.

Jessica had been assembling a puzzle of a scene from productive life while she worked at her husband's office. At the same time her mind was putting together a very different puzzle picture of a new creative life.

With each "centerpiece" Jessica was making mental preparations to draw and paint. Arranging and rearranging the objects on the cloth gave her an opportunity to practice her compositional skills. The appreciation from visitors to the office built her self-confidence as an artist.

Jessica's work situation wasn't typical, but even with her very flexible schedule she hadn't recognized the gift of time and space available to pursue her creative interests.

After a few seconds of silence, she returned from her reverie. The rest of the hour we focused on how she could be more intentional about using her hours at the office to allow two or three time slots for painting every workday. Her husband's office doubled nicely as a day studio. Her centerpieces, so carefully constructed with an artist's eye, brought calm to her husband's clients and could do the same for Jessica as she entered into the joyful process of drawing and painting. Future viewers of her watercolors, should she decide to do a series and exhibit them, could enjoy the centering quality of the images too. Classic both/and.

Having a "day job" doesn't mean you can't have time for your creative life. Use your lunch break to explore a new idea, read a chapter in a book related to your craft, make phone calls, order materials, meditate or check your progress on your long-term goals. Keep a notebook by your desk to record ideas.

Like a puzzle with two sides, our everyday lives and our creative lives exist simultaneously. There is always time and space for both.

Believe in the Power of "Good Enough"

Writers, think of a time when you finished reading a novel. Disgusted, you slammed the book on the end table and shouted, "I'm a better writer than that author! How does trash like that get published?" Here's how: The author submitted the work and the book fit the market. You can't sell unless you submit.

Artists, remember a time when you went to a gallery opening. The featured artist stood in a circle of smiling guests sipping white wine. You wandered the periphery of the gallery eyeing the paintings, many with red Sold stickers. You muttered under your breath, "I'm a better painter than this artist! How did she get a show?! " Easy, the artist submitted a proposal to the gallery, presented works for consideration, and painted enough pieces to fill the gallery. You can't sell unless you show.

You have to participate in the life you want to live. It won't just happen. Forget the romantic notion of getting discovered. Novels in drawers and paintings under the bed don't get discovered. Writers and artists, who do creative work, submit their work for consideration, and follow-through to complete their contracts or agreements by deadline do enjoy some measure of success. Take action, get results.

Release your work into the marketplace and trust the process. Some paintings and books will sell and others will not, but you can't predict which will and which won't. It takes confidence in your creative abilities and courage to take a risk. Don't say "This will never sell." You don't know that. Let other people make their own decisions. Don't assume an agent won't like your story, assume she might! Don't assume your paintings are not marketable; assume the right buyer is out there looking for a painting. Don't assume you're not good enough to compete. You are.

Assume your efforts today are good enough for today, then get up again tomorrow morning and try again. Create your work and let your work speak for itself. The world deserves a chance to see what you can do. Trust the process and trust the public. You may be surprised.

We're all in the learning process. Allow some grace in your life. Exercise a little faith, but have faith in a positive outcome, not a negative outcome. Don't give into fear and perfectionism, the power of good enough will give you the courage to release your creative energies to the world.

Don't Quit Your Day Job

Steve, a classically trained musician, planned to drive to Tulsa on Thursday afternoon to meet for coaching over dinner. I suggested my favorite restaurant, Lola's at the Bowery. In view of Tulsa's downtown skyline, the restaurant has a New York City look and feel. On Thursday nights, Lola books live entertainment, a perfect location for a musician to get a new perspective on his life.

Lola and I have been friends for almost thirty years. I arrived early to allow some time to visit with her before Steve arrived. After introductions Lola walked us across the dining room to a table by the big bay window.

"You have an hour of quiet. The band won't be setting up for Rebecca for a while."

"Rebecca Ungerman?" Steve asked.

Lola nodded as she seated us at a table for two by the big bay window. "You must be a jazz man to know our Tulsa Diva!"

"Steve, tell me what you like about jazz," I said.

"I love the way the music evolves and changes and the freedom the musicians seem to enjoy."

Freedom. I'd received my first clue about Steve's needs. Lola's daughter, Jennie, arrived with glasses of water and menus. "Steve, this is Lola's daughter, Jennie."

Steve leaned towards me while making eye contact with Jennie; he whispered loudly enough for her to hear, "She's as beautiful as her mother."

Jennie shyly smiled her big dazzling smile, pointed out a couple of favorite entrees on the menus and left us to make our selections.

"Steve, would you tell me a little about your job?"

"I'm a church musician. I play for three worship services each Sunday, choir practice every Wednesday night and occasional funerals and weddings. My job is only part-time but it keeps me busy."

"Tell me what you enjoy about your job."

"I like music and I like performing. The sanctuary piano and organ are magnificent instruments and the acoustics are amazing; but after all these years I'm tired of the same music over and over. I'm thinking about a job change."

"How long have you worked as a church organist?"

"Sixteen years."

"Are there any other problems with your job besides your boredom?"

"There's pressure to make each service perfect. Music is a huge draw for members and potential members. The expectations are high."

Steve worked for a prestigious non-denominational church in another city. He was essentially a long-term contract employee with benefits. The part-time pay was adequate for his expenses and allowed him an abundance of free time, which I suspected he was not using to his creative advantage. I needed to know about his other interests.

"Steve, how do you channel your extra creativity?"

"What do you mean by extra creativity?"

"Most creative people need a variety of creative outlets outside of their day jobs. Every once in a while a job will manifest purpose and self-actualization, but many creative people supplement their jobs with other creative work and interests."

"What's your day job, Romney?"

"I teach art in the public school."

"Tell me, what do you do with your extra creativity, besides teaching and coaching?" Steve asked wryly.

"Touché!" We both laughed. "Well, Steve, I write and I paint. I write at home and I rent a small studio space in town for painting."

"That sounds like a lot of irons in many fires!"

"I guess I must like irons!"

Steve shook his head and chuckled. "Seriously, don't you feel spread a bit thin?"

"Occasionally, but I have a high need for creative variety, so I provide it for myself. Taking care of my creative needs is *my* job. It's my job to feed my creativity. It's not the job of my employer to make sure I'm creatively challenged. I've learned it's unrealistic to think that one job, any job, would be enough to keep a truly creative person challenged indefinitely."

"Back up a minute." Steve leaned across the table, "Are you saying I shouldn't expect to feel artistically challenged by my work?"

"By your work, yes; by your job, not necessarily. There's a difference. Your work is your music or whatever other creative thing you choose to do. Your job is to play for church services."

"You're mincing words." Steve looked skeptical.

"Maybe a bit." I smiled in hopes of softening the conversation. "Let me ask you a question. When you first started playing at the church were you challenged by the music?"

"Oh yes, there was a lot to learn."

"Did you enjoy learning the new music?"

"Sure I did."

"Now that you know the music, the challenge is gone, right?"

"Definitely."

"Maybe this is why you are thinking about leaving your job. No challenge. You've mastered the music so you're bored."

"Isn't that reason enough to leave?" Steve's words had a slight defensive tone.

"It's *a* reason to leave, but it might also be a great reason to stay."

"How's that?"

"Steve, you're a professional. You've got job security and the church pays you well enough to cover your expenses, right?"

"Right."

"You're familiar enough with the music so that you probably don't have to practice mega hours to be prepared for Sunday anymore?"

Steve agreed.

"Your part-time job provides ample time for you to feel free to work on creative projects. So what challenges have you created for yourself?"

"Well, I'm working on some new musical compositions and I also write poetry."

"Have you been composing and writing lately?"

"No, I haven't." Steve looked out the window and watched a couple walk arm-in-arm down the sidewalk. He spoke softly, "For several months now I've been feeling too depressed about my job to do much else."

"Maybe the two are related."

Our entrees arrived and we stopped talking for a while to enjoy a few bites of the delicious curry chicken.

"Steve, what kind of music are you writing?"

"I've created variations on classical themes, compositions that sound like emotions or the seasons. I describe it as poetry set to music."

"And you're a poet too?" I asked.

"Well, I wasn't planning on talking about that, but yes, I write poetry. I got a music degree with a minor in English. Poetry feeds my soul. It's my secret passion."

"Which poets do you like to read?"

"Taylor Mali is one of my favorites. You would enjoy his poem "What Teachers Make.""

"I would like to read that one. What other poets do you read?"

"I like David Whyte for my more thoughtful moods and Rumi for insights into the spiritual side of life. I used a David Whyte poem called "The Well of Grief" as the starting point for one of my compositions."

"I'd like to read the poem and hear your piece."

Steve's eyes brightened a bit. "I wish I knew the poem by heart, but here's the essence," he thought for a moment, "Whyte's poem creates an image of coins thrown into a wishing well drifting down through the water. That's the sound I'm trying to create in my piano composition."

"That's more challenging than teaching art to kids! Have you heard music that conveys an image like that?"

"Franz Liszt. His compositions were called Symphonic Poems."

"This is fascinating! Have you performed your compositions?"

"No, I'm just not ready. I've got a dozen or so compositions in process. They're nowhere near ready to perform."

"Will you make recordings?"

"Someday, when they're ready."

Someday was a red-flag word. Someday never comes. "What's keeping you from getting them ready?" I asked.

Steve leaned across the table, "My perfectionism, I guess. What I want is to do is play my pieces all the way through start to finish, just as I would in a concert, but I freeze up somewhere in the middle. That's when I quit and start over. When the music doesn't sound the way I want it to, I get frustrated and stop."

"Then what do you do?"

"I usually decide to practice Sunday's music."

"So when you get discouraged, you do more of the very thing that bores you?"

"I hadn't thought about that way, but I guess you're right. That's incredibly sad, isn't it?" Steve sighed and sipped his drink. "I'm impatient with myself. I want my music to be perfect and until it is, I won't be satisfied."

Steve crossed his arms over this chest and leaned back in his chair. "I want to play my own music in one continuous, perfect stream. That's how a concert has to be. I've had performances that were perfect a time or two before so I know it's possible."

"Chasing the magic feeling, huh?"

He nodded, "All the time."

"There's a chance you're letting an unrealistic expectation keep you from realizing your creative dream."

"Why is it unrealistic? I play seamlessly every Sunday in church!"

"And your pieces are hymns or solos lasting only a few minutes each."

"Yes, and I play them perfectly. It can be done." Steve was resolute.

"Maybe your compositions could be played perfectly if there were short breaks in between pieces? You know, the order of a worship service has the music interspersed throughout with prayers, songs and a sermon. What do you do in those pauses?"

"I gather my thoughts and prepare to play again," he said.

Jennie refilled my glass of iced tea and I took a sip, "If you're used to some breaks in the service, couldn't you build some breaks into your performance to recreate those pauses so you could feel more confident and less stressed?"

Steve considered this question while he took a bite of his Ensalada Caprese. "What could I put in the breaks?" Steve stopped abruptly and leaned forward across the table, "Poetry! I could have poetry readings in between my pieces. A poem could be read before I played my matching composition. I could choose poems to complement my compositions. That's a great idea!"

"It was your idea," I said with a smile, "You're the one who knows about poetry and music."

"I could even include a few of my own poems. All I need now is a great reader."

"For your live performances and CD recording?"

"Yes!" Steve pulled out a small notebook out of his coat pocket and began scribbling notes. I looked at what he was writing; he wasn't working on a resume. Steve never even looked up when I ordered decaf coffee for two.

Steve's day job wasn't his real problem. His job wasn't *keeping* him from doing his creative work. Steve had just neglected to tend his own creative fires. Steve's vocation was church organist, but his avocation was musician and a poet. Music and words fed his creative inner fire.

Steve blamed his work for his mood and also for his inability to perform perfectly. He'd made his job mean more in his life than it should have; a job is just a job. A job can be replaced with another one.

Denzel Washington said his favorite motto was "Do what you got to do so that you can do what you want to do." Steve finally understood that his job was what he "…got to do so he could do what he wanted to do"—compose music, write poetry, and perform.

Steve's current state of mind was the result of his own inaction. Somewhere along the way, he'd stopped challenging himself as a musician. He'd put out his own creative fire by adopting unrealistically high expectations for his own performance.

As we continued our discussion over coffee, Steve realized his job at the church was an asset, not a liability. We listed several plusses: the church provided top-of-the-line instruments, an acoustically perfect "concert hall," and a congregation full of ready-made fans. The church could also advertise and promote his poetry and music concerts at no cost to Steve. He could look forward to playing to a house full of potential buyers of his CD which would generate extra income to fund more of his creative pursuits.

Even after sixteen years and counting, Steve hadn't realized his job provided time for him to freely pursue his interests in composition and poetry—all he had to do was use that time to his advantage.

As we drank coffee and listened to Rebecca Ungerman work her magic, I watched Steve resolve to allow his life to evolve and change—just like jazz.

Creative Business Planning

Creative people often prefer to walk to the beat of a different drummer—especially when it comes to setting business goals and practices. While the fancy leather planning calendars and color-coded filing systems look enticing in the Sunday ads, they usually remain unused by right-brained creative adults.

In a workshop on combating procrastination and perfectionism, an admitted perfectionist asked for a sure way to make sure she met a deadline. "I don't have a problem starting a project, I have a problem stopping. I never know when I'm done. I just keep working on my project. I add, I subtract, I edit, I start over. I unravel what I've done! How can I quell this feeling that whatever I've done still needs more work?"

Bless her heart. When I was a child my mother used to be my "stopper." She would drop in to look at my drawing and tell me when to quit. I eventually learned to trust her judgment enough to comply.

My suggestion for the constant unraveler: set a deadline that is so public you would be too embarrassed to ask for an extension. For artists wanting to get back to painting I suggest they book a show. Commercial galleries and colleges and university galleries set their show schedules many months in advance. Once the date is set, it's not easily changed. The deadline can never be pushed so far back onto your brain's back burner that you'll be able to forget about it. Your awareness of your responsibility to produce quality work will grow larger each day.

An artist's reputation is on the line when a show is booked. If you fail to produce the work and if you don't present it show-ready by the deadline you may never get another chance to redeem yourself. Most serious artists realize what's riding on a show and will nearly kill themselves to have everything ready on time. My oldest son worked around the clock for nearly three days getting everything in order for his Senior Show opening at William Woods University. His room-sized installation piece was spectacular and worth every minute of lost sleep!

Writers can set short-term goals by joining a critique group. Each week the group expects your participation. Of course, you can drop out, but you may not be asked back into the group in the future. When a writer sets a long-term goal such as a date to mail in a manuscript—the pressure is on. Calling the date that your work is due a *deadline* underlines the importance of the date.

It takes courage to state a goal publicly. It takes determination to develop a plan to meet that goal. Once you make a commitment to actually do what you say you will do you're also agreeing to put a stop to the chit-chat, dreaming, and excuse making. You have to say "This is the day. Now is the right time. I know enough to begin."

There's no reason to dwell on the times when you've lost opportunities or times when you said you would start and you did not. Forget all that. Even God can't change the past! Call me if you need an "official" absolution from an ordained minister and I'll forgive your sin of procrastination! Choose to live in the present moment and look forward.

Develop a plan to ensure your efforts will net real, measurable results. Every action you take needs to systematically move you toward your goal one day at a time. The forward movement creates momentum and builds your confidence. Some basics about creative business plans:

1.   Your plan must be simple.
2.   Your long-term plan must have some built in wiggle-room for family emergencies or illness.
3.   Your plan must make sense to you. You must believe it is achievable.

4.   Your plan must fit you. You're not making a plan for a business guru with dozens of staff members. Your plan is usually for you alone, although collaboration on a book can bring other people into your goal planning and artists committed to a group show must work together as they plan.

5.   Revisit your plan weekly to keep it fresh in your mind. Post your goal where you can see it daily. Most any surface will do. Post a note on your computer, medicine cabinet mirror or refrigerator door.

Here's how I coach my clients to create a personalized business plan. The basic premise is this:

GOAL + PLAN + TIME = SUCCESS.

•   **Materials needed:** A month by month calendar for reference, a pen, and a packet of sticky notes.

•   **Time required:** About an hour.

Romney's Twelve Step Business Plan for Creative People

1.   **State your goal.** For example: "I will have 3 chapters written on my book (use the working title for your book) by the end of April" or "I will have two completed paintings gallery-ready by the end of April."

2.   **Define a time frame:** Set a relatively short time frame. One to three months is long enough to get something done and yet is a short enough time to keep from feeling overwhelmed. To make your deadline finish line date more memorable, choose to complete your goal on a special day worthy of celebration such as your birthday or a national holiday. Notable days are always foremost in our minds and such days are easily remembered.

3.   **Define the total time frame by dividing into weeks:** Write on several sticky notes:

•   "Week 1, April 1-7."

•   "Week 2, April 8-14," etc.

Make one sticky note for each week all the way to the end of your time frame.

4. **Arrange these notes on a tabletop (in calendar order from left to right or from top to bottom with the closest week at the top and the last week at the bottom). Leave space below or beside each "week" note for additional notes.**

5. **Brainstorm all the steps or tasks you can think of that will be required to complete the task you've chosen.** Write each task on a separate sticky note.

    Tasks may include:

    - **Work time**: Commit to a total number of hours per week that will work. You might designate every Saturday to work. You might prefer more manageable chunks of time spread out over the week. If you have been off task for some time working three to five hours per week may be enough to get started. As your project progresses and you fall more in love with it, you'll want to increase your time.

    - **Research time:** You'll spend some time reading or researching a particular subject. Don't spend too much time on the Internet; remember research librarians love to help patrons. Build in time for trips to the library or to the gallery where you'll be showing your work.

    - **Contact time:** Creative projects will require phone calls, appointments, email exchanges, etc.

    - **Re-energizing time:** Every creative person needs some time to re-charge their mental energies. Writers would enjoy an occasional afternoon in a bookstore. Artists would relish a walk though a local museum.

6. **Place all the "task" sticky notes beside the week in which you think you will do the task.** Realize that it is difficult to project that far into the future but some tasks will naturally fall into the beginning of the project like writing a query letter to a publisher or calling to schedule a show. Other tasks will naturally occur later in the process,

such as finding someone to edit your writing or ordering frames and invitations.

7.   **Place all the notes on a big sheet of paper or poster board.** Visual thinkers appreciate this extra-large hand-made calendar. Feel free to personalize it with markers or photos. Being able to see the big picture, one to three months on a single sheet of paper, will help you focus. The physical act of creating a calendar specifically for this project will also give special meaning to your goal and plan.

8.   **Hang the calendar in your workspace or in a space you see every day.**

9.   **Get to work on the tasks that you determined were needed to be done first.** Write your query letter, don't do research.

10.   **Record your daily and weekly time totals.** Give yourself a pat on the back. It's affirming to see the number of hours you've worked and what you've accomplished. If tasks take longer than you think or delays arise, simply shift that sticky note to the next week and keep on working. At the end of your time frame, celebrate your efforts!

11.   **Check your progress at the same time each week.** Monday or Friday check-ins work well for most people.

12.   **Make revisions as needed.** As you think of other tasks, it's easy to add them to your calendar. There's always room for one more sticky note.

PART II:
Straight Talk for Creative People

Talking to Yourself: Self-Coaching Basics

Clients usually come to a coaching appointment with a creative quandary or question such as, "Why do I say I want to write a book, but I do everything but write?" or "How do I get out of this creative slump so I can paint again?" or "My partner doesn't understand my creative work. How can I move on without his approval?"

My job as a creativity coach is to ask the next right question to help my client find his or her own answer. Once a solution is found, then we work together to develop a workable plan to ensure measurable successes over time.

I'm convinced most people can coach themselves through their own problems and find workable solutions. I know it sounds as if I'm talking myself out of a job, but it's true: you can coach yourself. I firmly believe if an individual has thought about his or her problem thoroughly enough to form a single question and ask for advice, that person already knows the answer—he or she only lacks the confidence to trust and act on that inner knowledge.

To be your own coach you must:

1. Trust your ability to positively influence your thinking and actions. Have you ever thrown yourself a pity party? Then you've successfully influenced yourself negatively. Can you pull yourself up by your bootstraps and get something done when you're in a pinch? Most of us can. It's called self-confidence, bravado, guts or sheer nerve. In self-coaching you must be willing to positively influence yourself.

2. Openly communicate with yourself. To coach yourself you must be willing to examine your answers objectively. You will have to be honest with yourself and be willing to be "beside yourself" in order to ask yourself the next logical question. The answer will move you to the next step. You know your habits, patterns of thinking, denial systems, and personal motivations. You *can* be your own coach.

3.   Honestly chart your progress over time. Do you try to meet deadlines or do you make excuses for inaction? What would motivate you to push to meet a deadline, make a phone call, or send out a query letter?

4.   Have a vision for your future that is clear, measurable, and personally enticing. Do you know what you want? Have you ever visualized yourself at a book signing with a line of well-wishers waiting for your signature? Can you see yourself at a gallery opening greeting new patrons who are admiring your painting or sculpture? Can you imagine standing on the stage of Carnegie Hall looking at a sold-out audience?

What about becoming a guest on the Oprah show to discuss your latest book? This is my personal dream. To make it more real in my own mind, while on a holiday in New York City, my husband and I visited Madame Tussauds Wax Museum. "Oprah" was one wax figure and of course, I had my picture taken with the wax "her." In the photo she looks quite happy to meet me! To inspire my artistic side I also had my photo taken with Picasso, Salvador Dali and Andy Warhol. To enrich my intellect I stood thoughtfully next to Einstein. For an extra blessing I stood close to the Dali Lama and Billy Graham.

Take opportunities to make your dreams real in your mind and heart. Take an hour to sketch a design for your book cover. Wrap your cover over another book and pretend you're holding your latest release. Feel free to put your name in the top of the page and the title at the bottom of the page like a literary star! This exercise will give you a concrete gesture to help make your dreams of being a published writer come true. Find creative and imaginative ways to feed your dreams and fuel your goals and plans. Focus your thoughts and efforts on what you want. Dream big! You have nothing to lose!

5.   To move forward you must be able to self-start, take responsibility for your dreams and work steadily toward them. Don't leave your future up to chance. Be willing to

develop a plan. State your dreams and anticipate doors opening before you.

Who are the movers and shakers who could catapult your career? I'd like to meet Dr. Wayne Dyer and Oprah, of course. I'm already visualizing each of them holding this book and reading it. On a piece of paper write the names of the people you want to know about you and your creative work. Post the list of names by your workspace. Your wish could move them into your path!

6.   Be self-regulating. You must be willing to notice and manage your thoughts and actions. Keep your thoughts in the realm of the positive. See your inner coach as a partner and friend able to recognize your mood swings and shifts in attention that could derail your creativity.

If you choose to be an active observer of your life you'll recognize when you begin to slip into periods of low energy due to apathy or negative thinking. Be a friend to yourself and take immediate action to realign your thoughts back into positive realms. Do you need to go for a walk outside to clear your thoughts or spend time in quiet meditation and prayer? What do you do to restore balance and to regain your enthusiasm and productivity?

When you take charge of your life you know how to reenergize your thinking and creativity, you don't look to someone else to do that for you. You are a creative adult, willing to chide or congratulate yourself as needed.

Exercise: How to become your own creativity coach

Perhaps you have a trusted counselor, psychologist, therapist or clergy person. When you come to the point of calling for an appointment you're admitting, "I have a problem. I trust you can help me work through it." This is an attitude of coach-ability. You're willing to ask for and take advice.

Our family has a trusted counselor. I value his opinions and expertise. He's an excellent listener and he's smart. I appreciate his ability to cut to the chase. What I admire most is his ability to ask the next right question. He is one of my models for coaching.

When I make a counseling appointment I arrive on time. I've done my mental and emotional homework. I'm able to articulate my problem and I'm ready to listen. Experience tells me that when my fifty minutes are over I'll have an action plan.

You have an inner coach that is knowledgeable about you, your habits and patterns of behavior. To be your own coach you must separate yourself into two parts: your ordinary self and your "inner creativity coach."

Separating yourself is something we do without realizing it. You've probably heard someone say, "I was beside myself with worry," "I can't stand myself," or "I gave myself a good talking-to." These comments indicate our very human ability to see a part of ourselves as a separate entity. When you engage in self-talk, you're "talking to yourself." Too often, our self-talk is negative. Use your innate ability to influence your thinking in positive ways. Build yourself up rather than tearing yourself down.

The basic requirements for becoming your own coach are intelligence, courage and common sense. Don't waste any more time regretting the past when you didn't write or paint. Confess your truth to yourself and get into conversation with your inner coach.

Begin by setting aside at least twenty minutes for your self-coaching session. Find a quiet private place where you can talk to yourself aloud without anyone else overhearing or noticing. Place two chairs face to face for this self-coaching session. Two kitchen chairs across from each other would be fine. One chair is reserved for your inner coach; the other chair is for you. Get up and change seats when your conversation switches from you to your inner coach and back again. I urge you to make these actual physical moves from chair to chair—it really helps keep the momentum going strong. Don't be tempted to make notes while you're self-coaching. Slowing down to make notes breaks the flow and encourages self-editing. Keep your coaching session completely verbal—just like a real session with your therapist. Just talk with yourself—quickly and honestly.

Take a moment to verbalize your real "Why?" question before beginning. "Why am I not writing, painting, or acting?" "Why am

I afraid to start a new project?" "Why do I hate my job but don't look for another job?" Ask the real "Why?" question and then honestly answer the question. Your verbal exchange between you and your coach might sound like this:

You: "Why am I not writing my novel?" (Switch seats)

Your inner coach: "I don't know, you tell me. Why aren't you writing your novel?" (Go back to your original seat)

You: "Well, I'm afraid." (Switch seats)

Your inner coach: "What are you afraid of?" (Switch seats)

You: "What if I can't finish it?"

Your inner coach: "What if you can't start it?"

You: "I haven't started it."

Your inner coach: "So, if you can't start it, then you certainly can't finish it, can you?"

You: "Gosh, you're tough. I thought coaches were supposed to be supportive."

Your inner coach: "I could be supportive if you'd give me something to work with here. Write something, anything, and I'll be plenty supportive."

You: "I have been journaling."

Your inner coach: "Journaling is writing, but you've been journaling for years. You know your writing teacher considers journaling self-indulgent. Why don't you start a story, develop some characters, solve a mystery, or stir up a romance. I'm tired of hearing your inner musings, they're going nowhere fast."

You: "You're right. I've been journaling instead of working on a structured story for too many years."

Your inner coach: "Exactly. Don't waste any more valuable time. Isn't there a story hidden somewhere in your journal that you could use as a starting point for a short story or something?"

You: "Maybe. I could read through some old journals and see what's in there."

Your inner coach: "Well, don't spend more than a couple of hours leafing through that stack of journals. The goal is to start writing, remember?"

You: "You're right. My goal is to start writing."

Your inner coach: "So, start right now. Prove to me you can. Tell me a story about your mother, or your dog or your next door neighbor."

You: "Okay. 'My mother's next door neighbor had a Cocker Spaniel named Marie.'"

Your inner coach: "I'm interested. Why did she name the dog, Marie?"

You: "Because her favorite show was *Everybody Loves Raymond*. Marie was Raymond's mother."

Your inner coach: "That was a great show. What happened to Marie the dog?"

You: "My mother accidentally ran over Marie with her new SUV."

Your inner coach: "Excuse me for laughing, but that's sad and funny. Okay, I'm convinced you can write a complete sentence in English. Now, how are you going to help yourself get on track with your writing goals? What are you going to do *today*?"

You: "I'm going to write my novel."

Your inner coach: "Why not take some of the heat off and not say the word "novel." Commit to something less stressful like writing twenty minutes a day for starters. Would that be so hard?"

You: "That's very reasonable. I can do that."

Your inner coach: "Doesn't writing twenty minutes a day sound less frightening than saying you're going to write a novel?"

You: "Yes, it does sound less intimidating."

Your inner coach: "You look less stressed too. When will you write?"

You: "I don't know, just sometime during the day."

Your inner coach: "No. That's not a good enough answer. I want to know *when* you're going to sit in front of your computer and writer for twenty minutes—exactly when."

You: "How about 4:00-4:20 p.m.?"

Your inner coach: "That sounds fine. Are you going to write seven days a week or only five?"

You: "I can commit to six."

Your inner coach: "Twenty minutes a day, seven days a week would be so much better. You wouldn't have a chance for your ideas to get cold. Come on, how about seven days a week?"

You: "Oh, all right, you've convinced me."

Your inner coach: "Great! This is a great start. Speaking of starting, you will start today won't you?"

You: "This afternoon."

Your inner coach: "Great! I'm proud of you. You've set a reasonable goal and you're willing to start today. Today is always the right day to begin. Now, I think we should set up our next appointment now—just to keep you accountable. Next week, same time?"

You: "You drive a hard bargain, but I'll agree. Next week, same time. Thanks for your help."

In my creativity classes I give my students fifteen-minutes to have a self-coaching session on the first night of class. My purpose is to help my students discover their creative blocks or nail their excuses for inaction. They must follow my directions completely—all the way to changing seats with each response. There's something about getting up and down that jars your brain into honesty. A self-coaching session won't take long—fifteen or twenty minutes are usually sufficient for your inner coach to get your real self back on track. Talking to yourself really works. Give it a try.

Time Out

The topic for the evening's class was time management. I wrote on the board: GOAL + PLAN + TIME = SUCCESS. As I handed each student a packet of colored pencils and a one-page calendar of the next eighteen months I said, "Here are the instructions: Write your goal across the top of this calendar. Your goal should be ten words or less. You may use any color you like."

The artsy students dumped their pencils out on the table top like pick-up sticks. Others carefully pulled out one pencil out at a time examining their choices. Some started writing right away while others were carefully considering the wording of their goal statement, counting words. Having both time and materials, the adults thoroughly enjoyed coloring.

After a few minutes I looked at their artistic goal statements. A couple had drawn a frame-like border around their sentence. One used a different color for each of her block letters.

"Circle today's date." I said. "Today is the best day to begin working toward your goal. Now choose the date you want as your deadline and circle it."

The students looked up, startled...deer-in-the-headlight eyes.

"Choose right now the deadline for your project. By what date do you want to reach your goal?"

Most frowned as if I'd asked them to solve a story problem.

"I'll give you a couple of minutes to choose a date." I waited and waited. When a supervisor sets a deadline that person is just doing his or her job, but to set your own deadline sometimes feels stressful.

Don had circled a date three months out. "Don, could we use you goal and plan and deadline to get us started?"

"Yeah. Sure."

I reviewed what we knew about Don's goal. "He wants a short story. His plan is for the story to have 10,000 words. His target deadline date is three months out from today. Don's deadline is a real date on his calendar, not "someday."

I pointed again to the board. "GOAL + PLAN + TIME = SUCCESS. "Time in the equation refers to time spent on the project—daily time and calendar time. It takes time to write, paint, practice or clean out a house."

I instructed the class to color in all the days leading up to their deadline. This created a visual block of time with a beginning and end. The purpose was to instill value to each day. In color, every day counted.

"Time for some simple math. Ten thousand words divided by twelve should give us a word count goal for each week. "Who has a calculator?" Ellen, the only left-brained student in the class, pulled a small calculator out of her purse.

Ellen and her teenage daughter Laura sat side by side in the second row. Both were beautiful blonds. Ellen's hair was sculpted into in a French twist. She looked like a petite Tippi Hedren from Hitchcock's movie, *Marnie*. Laura's thick braid fell halfway down her back. She was a dancer.

The first night of class Ellen told us about her family. Everyone was well organized and capable of sequential thinking—all except Laura, the creative soul. Ellen enrolled in the class for insights into the creative personality. Laura was a freshman at a highly ranked high school where the homework load was heavy. Ellen tattled on Laura saying she rarely finished her homework before midnight. Laura claimed homework was "not a problem" for her—only for her mother.

Like any teenager, Laura put her "real" life before her homework. She preferred to use her after school hours for what really mattered: hobbies, friends, TV, and text messaging—homework was way down on the list. Ellen hoped some of my time management strategies would help Laura operate more efficiently. Even as the youngest member of the class, Laura felt at home in our class of creative adults. Ellen was the odd man out, but she was a good sport about it. She simply wanted her daughter to be more self-regulating and proactive about her schoolwork. I could sympathize.

I motioned toward Ellen, "We've got our accountant." The class applauded. We were relieved to be free of the anxiety of doing long division the old-fashioned way. Ellen smiled and took a mini-bow by tipping her head. Happy to be in her element, her polished nails flew over the calculator buttons.

"833 words a week," Ellen said.

"Don," she asked, "Do you want to write seven days a week or write five days a week with your weekends off?"

"I think five days a week."

Ellen had the next set of calculations in a flash.

"166."

Greg, our mystery writer gasped, "A day? Only one hundred and sixty six words *a day?*"

This was so much less work than anyone expected.

"Well, actually," Ellen corrected, "166 words times five days a week times twelve weeks equals 9960 words. That's a little less than Don's goal of 10,000 words."

Still, we were astounded.

"Is that even a *page?*" Laura blurted.

"Not quite," I said, "a full page double spaced is about 250 words."

"How many *lines* is that?" Laura was interested.

"About twelve," Ellen, our efficiency expert said.

I restated the obvious, "Half a page five days a week for three months will net Don one short story."

"Even *I* could do that!" Laura said. Don glanced at Laura.

"Sure you could. Any writer could manage twelve lines a day," I said.

"But I want twelve *good* lines and that could take a lot of time," said Don.

"Yes, that's true. The problem is not *if* you could write twelve lines. You can. The real question you have to consider is this: How much time every day are you willing to allot to the process of writing those twelve *good* lines?" This was my entrée into time management. "Even a few minutes a day adds up."

I gave each student my handout.

Ten Steps and Twenty Minutes a Day to Meet Your Goal

1. Buy a digital timer.
2. Prepare your work space:
   - Clear your workspace of any clocks.
   - Put a sticky note over the clock in the corner of your computer screen.
   - Take off your watch.
   - No TV (we know how long a TV show lasts).
   - No radio either (Dee jays report the time).
   - If the sound of silence is too loud, choose a quiet instrumental CD. The idea is to create a time-free and word-free workspace. To operate at your maximum creativity, take away the awareness of time and let your right brain play.
3. Sit down and put your fingers on the keyboard, hold your paintbrush, or pull your guitar strap over your neck and put your fingers on the chord. Do whatever you do to put your body in the "work" position.
4. Set the digital timer for twenty minutes.
5. Take a deep breath, exhale and press "start."
6. Start doing your creative work and don't stop until the timer beeps. Don't leave your workspace unless there is a fire or someone is bleeding at your door. If your cat comes in for a tummy rub ignore him. If the phone rings, let it roll

to voice mail. Stay put for the full time and work. The world can go on without your input for twenty minutes.

7.   When the beeper beeps, reset it for five minutes. You are now on a five-minute "break." Leave your workplace. Do something unrelated to your creative work. In five minutes you can unload a dishwasher, open mail, get a drink of water, or walk outside.

8.   When the timer beeps at the end of five minutes go back to your workspace and sit down.

9.   Reset the timer for twenty minutes, press the start button, and get back to work.

10.   Repeat the process as needed.

The structure of twenty minutes on and five minutes off focuses your efforts into short spurts of energy and creativity. You'll be surprised how much you can accomplish.

Twenty minutes is a manageable length of time to focus your attention on a single task. Without mental or physical distractions, you should be able to give your full attention to your work. Devoting quality time and attention to your project proves that your work matters. Our time is valuable. Even twenty minutes is valuable.

This 20/5 game will work for most any task. Does your garage need cleaning but you can't find a free day? Set your timer and sort through a corner of the garage for twenty minutes. Is it time to go through your closet and donate clothes? Set your timer for twenty minutes. Twenty minutes of reading every day on a favorite subject will make you an expert. Twenty minutes of listening to your first grader read aloud will make her a confident reader. Twenty-minute increments of homework with five-minute breaks for phone chats will get homework done before midnight too. Twenty minutes is enough to make a difference.

I'll point out the obvious: You can't write a novel while you're mowing the lawn. You can't paint a portrait while you're doing the dishes. You can only *think about* it. You can't do your creative work while you are doing something else. You must be in your workspace. You have to put your seat in the seat.

After break I asked Don, "Do you think you could write twelve good lines in twenty minutes or forty minutes?"

Don's body posture looked like Rodin's "The Thinker." He didn't answer my question.

He didn't come back to class the next week.

I regret I didn't have a chance to talk to Don about eudemonia. Aristotle coined the term. It means a feeling of joy or fulfillment that arises from taking meaningful action. What's meaningful? That's up to you. Meaningful actions may eventually lead to a desired goal, and in the meantime there is a real pleasure to be found in the action itself.

The action may be pounding out twelve lines every day on the keyboard, stretching a canvas for a new painting, or rehearsing a guitar riff until you can play it with ease. The good feeling comes from actually doing even the smallest piece of something that matters to you. That good feeling can happen in twenty minutes a day too. It's the old "life is a journey, not a destination" idea. Doing what gives you pleasure is enough reason to do it. If you enjoy writing, you'll enjoy crafting a perfect phrase. If painting is fun, slapping gesso on canvas will be fun. If creating a scrapbook for your children gives you joy, you'll like sorting photos.

You do things all day long every day. You might as well do something that brings you joy and a sense of accomplishment. Even if you can only squeeze in twenty minutes a day, you'll look forward to it. At the end of the day it feels good to point to the work you've done and say, "Look what I did today!" GOAL + PLAN + TIME = SUCCESS (and joy, fun, satisfaction, pleasure etc.).

For Don to write a short story, he will have to sit in front of his computer and write. I wonder if he's writing or mowing?

Right Action, Right Time

They called themselves the Arkansas Romancers, but I'll always think of them as the "Ya-Ya" Writers.

Kayla called to ask if I did group coaching. "My writers group would like to have you talk to us."

"Would you tell me about your group?"

"Well, we're a small group of writers—only four. We're not an actual club, just a group of women friends who help each other tackle writing problems. We meet a couple of times a year for a few days of intensive writing and brainstorming. I read the description of your class on creative blocks in the Tulsa Community College course catalog and thought you might be able to help. We're staying at a hotel in Tulsa. Could you join us Thursday evening?"

When I arrived at the hotel, the women looked comfortable in their suite surrounded by salty snacks and plenty of chocolate. As soon as I walked in Kayla offered me a Diet Dr. Pepper. She moved a stack of newspapers aside and motioned me to take a seat on the sofa. She introduced me to her writing partners, Margaret and Dorothy and Dorothy's cousin, Dee.

As we were getting acquainted the phone rang. Dorothy answered. "Yes, I understand," she spoke calmly but firmly, "Yes, we are refusing housekeeping again today."

The women giggled as Dorothy hung up the phone. She looked at me and explained, "The management wanted to inform us that they were filling out an official report since we've refused housekeeping for three straight days." More laughter.

Dorothy waved her hand at the living area strewn with notebooks, sticky notes, pens, books and empty cups. "This is what 'refusing housekeeping' looks like, but we don't want to be disturbed, right girls?"

"Right!" the Romancers shouted in unison.

"Looks like home!" I slipped off my shoes and sat crossed legged on the too-firm hotel couch.

The Arkansas Romancers had been meeting together for several years. Sequestered from the world for a few days at a time, they helped each other become better writers. Margaret could outline a novel with ease. Kayla was an expert at writing love scenes. Dorothy was a master at fixing plot holes. Dee, a soon-to-be retired school librarian, was writing in the Young Adult fiction genre.

Together they hammered out the rough spots in each other's novels. These women did what Ya-Ya's do best—over the years they'd listened, laughed and loved each other as friends and as colleagues they'd helped each other reach increasing levels of success in the writing business.

"So, tell me, who wants to start?" I asked.

Margaret was seated closest to me. "I'll start." She clasped her hands and rested them on her knees. "I keep missing my deadlines. My agent is after me to get this book done."

"Her agent knows she'll get the novel done. She always gets it done. We can't figure out why she puts herself through the stress," Dorothy said.

Margaret shrugged. "I want to know why too," she said, "and I want to write more authentically, from my heart," she tapped her chest. "My dialogue seems cold. I'm not connecting with my heart." She pointed at Kayla, "She's the queen of romance dialogue. Beautiful sentences fall out of her fingers onto the keys. It's so easy for her." Kayla looked apologetically at Margaret.

"Margaret, tell me about your writing schedule."

"I don't have much of one these days."

"Have you had a writing schedule in the past that worked for you?"

She thought for a moment. "I used to write first thing in the morning until about eleven or so. After lunch I walked out to the barn to check on the horses. When I got back to the house, I wrote until about four."

"That sounds like a pretty productive day. What happened?"

"She's had some health problems," Kayla said.

"I'm better now, but I haven't gotten back to my old routine." Margaret said.

"Her new routine is to talk on the phone in the morning instead of writing," Dorothy tattled.

Margaret looked at Dorothy.

"Well, it's true," Dorothy said.

Margaret tried to explain, "I like to catch up with people in the morning. I have my coffee, check my email and call two or three friends. I probably spend more time on-line and on the phone than I should, but it makes me feel good to stay connected."

"How much time are we talking about here?"

"About an hour and a half to two hours."

"That's a lot of time."

"Yeah," she sighed, "It sounds worse now that we're talking about it."

"Do you write in the mornings now?"

"Yes, for a while until lunch and again sometimes in the late afternoon."

"Okay, let's think this through." I walked to the snack stash, considered my options and filled my Styrofoam bowl with Chex Mix.

"You feel like talking when you're rested and the whole day is ahead?" Margaret nodded. "And you say you have two problems, the first is not meeting your deadlines and the second is about wanting to write more authentic dialogue. What if both of these problems are connected? Both might be resolved by getting back to your old early morning writing schedule."

"How's that?" Dee asked for Margaret.

"Early morning is now your favorite time for connecting with your friends. That same time used to be your best time for writing. I'm guessing early morning is still your best time for writing because you seem to be alert and energetic. Your circadian rhythms are running high then," I explained.

"What kind of rhythms?" Margaret asked.

"Circadian," said Dee. "Your body has natural high and low energy swings during each twenty-four hour time period. You know, you have times when you feel with it and times when you feel out of it. I watch the kids at school cycle through a sleepy time right after lunch."

"You don't have to be a teenager to get sleepy after lunch. That's why I walk out to the pasture to check on my horses right after lunch. The fresh air wakes me up," Margaret said.

"Our bodies need activity and rest off and on during the day. Circadian cycles are different for each person. Some people are morning people and others are night people and then there are times off and on during the day when we have more energy than other times. These high-energy times are when the body is saying it's ready to work *with* you instead of *against* you. Most people have two or three peak performance times a day—usually one in the morning and another in the afternoon or evening," I said as I walked to the counter to refill my soft drink.

"Margaret, you told me your best times for writing used to be in the morning and midafternoon. Lunch time and immediately after was your low energy time. That's when you said you checked on the horses. After a little break and some fresh air you were ready to get back to work," I said.

"Your midday activities were restful and rejuvenating," said Dorothy.

"And didn't require much brain power," said Dee.

Group coaching seemed to be working.

"You already know your body's most efficient work schedule. Now all you have to do is get back in sync with it. I find most creative people waste their most productive time slots doing their least productive tasks, like chores and errands. Don't use your peak performance time on low priority activities," I said.

"Like talking on the phone or emailing friends," Kayla said.

"Your friends will be happy to talk with you later in the day or whenever," Dorothy said.

"Try writing again in the morning," I suggested as I settled back into the corner of the couch. "Call your friends and check your email later in the day instead of first thing in the morning."

"What did we do with all our time before email?" Dee mused, "It takes a lot of my time at school and at home."

"The Internet is a real trap for creative people! We're naturally curious and the web is a Pandora's box! I'm amazed how much time is wasted returning email and surfing the web. Writers who say they don't have time to write need to look at how much time they spend on line." I was almost on my soapbox when thankfully Margaret interrupted my lecture.

"What about my dialogue problem? How's that connected to an early morning work time?"

"I think it's all about timing, for you and your characters. You want to talk to your friends in the morning; maybe the characters in your book want to talk to you in the morning. How about giving your fictional friends a chance to get a word in?"

"What an interesting idea," Margaret tossed a handful of cashews into her mouth.

"Go back to your old writing schedule for a couple of weeks and see if it'll work for you again," Dee suggested.

"I've got nothing to lose but frustration," Margaret said.

Margaret discovered her high-energy time by paying attention to her body's natural flow of action and inaction. She listened to her body and heard it talking to her. Notice your daily highs and lows for a few days. Chart how you spend your time, when you feel energetic and when you feel a lull in energy. Your body is giving your clues so you can work with your body instead of against it.

Timing is everything—for Margaret and for the rest of us too. We know the old sayings about timing: "strike when the iron is hot" and "make hay while the sun shines." The Old Testament writer of Ecclesiastes expressed the same idea so beautifully: "To every thing there is a season, and a time to every purpose under the heaven."

Writers and creative people of all types can capitalize on their most valuable time by doing their creative work during their body's peak performance times. Don't tackle your hardest plot twist after lunch when you're feeling sleepy. Don't talk on the phone when your fingers are itching to write.

Choose the right time to work and guard your time by minimizing exterior distractions such as phone calls and email. When the phone rings let the voice mail take a message. You pay for the service, use it! A seminary professor on sabbatical had this voice mail message on her home phone: "Thanks for your call but

I'm writing now. I return calls between 4:30 and 5:00 each afternoon." That's how she got in a full day of uninterrupted writing time. Her strategy is worked for her in another way too. She told me, "By the time I got back to my callers, some no longer need to talk to me. They'd found someone else to solve their problem." Even better. Make yourself less available to work-time distractions.

Regarding email, while you're at work you may be expected to hit "reply" with lightening speed, but at home you can do what works for you. Choose to answer emails only once or twice a day. My home computer used to "ding" every time an email was received. I say "used to" because I turned the volume off on my computer so I can't hear the sound. I found I was compulsive enough that I felt the need to check my mail at every "ding." I lost my train of thought and valuable minutes of writing time. What a waste. Now I'm in charge of my work environment. My computer is there to serve me, not the other way around.

The opposite extreme of a "ding" is a friend's email alert system, he has a five-inch animated cartoon of a tuxedo-clad butler holding a letter on a silver tray. The butler walks across his screen, stops and turns to the viewer and announces purposefully in an English accent, "You have mail, sir." Every time the butler comes in the "room" my friend stops whatever he's doing, mumbles about the "damn interruption," and opens his email so he can "dismiss" the butler. Who's the boss?

Be an objective observer of your life and you'll find easy ways to improve your productivity. There is a right time for the right action.

Be Open to New Possibilities

Eric was a participant in one of my half-day creativity workshops held at a library. When class members stated their creative goals, Eric said he wanted to write a novel. At our first break, he asked if he could speak to me after the workshop.

At the end of the day Eric helped me gather my materials and helped load my car. We walked back into the library and stopped at the coffee bar for a snack. Eric got a cup of coffee and picked up a cookie. We went back in to the conference room and sat across from each other at a long table.

He began, "I'm a professional writer. I work for the newspaper." He looked tired as he stared into his coffee cup. "In just a few lines I can tell the reader who, what, where, when, why and even how, but the why question is the hardest one to answer." He tore open the powdered creamer and stirred the small mountains of white powder into his black coffee. Absently he asked, "How could anyone know why a person does one thing and not another?"

I waited while he gathered his thoughts.

"I've been in the same squeaky chair in the same crowded bull pen for twenty-three years. I'm extremely good at a job I hate."

"Is your job keeping you from writing your novel?" I asked.

"No, my job isn't the problem. The problem is that I write other people's stories when what I really want to do," he cleared his throat, "need to do, is write my dad's story." He looked absently around the empty room. "I've been talking about writing a novel for so many years even I'm bored with hearing me talking about it."

"So what's keeping you from writing?"

"Because it doesn't matter now if I do it or not. It's too late."

"Why is it too late?"

"Because my father passed away."

I was beginning to think I had missed some crucial part of the conversation.

"Is grief keeping you from writing?"

"Not grief, shame. It was his story and I promised him I would write it and I never got around to it." He looked down and spoke softly, "He died, still waiting for me to write his story. I let him down."

"But you still can write his story," I said.

"Yes, I know that, but I just can't seem to."

"Because you didn't keep your promise?"

"Yes, my father believed in me and I let him down. He was a war hero, for God's sake! Medals and everything. I'm ashamed that after all he did in his lifetime, I can't do this one little thing." Eric's voice trailed off as he put his head in his hands.

"Eric, writing a book is not a little thing. Writing is very hard work."

"And guilt only makes it harder," he said softly.

Eric needed an empathetic listener more than he needed a coach.

"Tell me your dad's story."

He pushed the metal chair back a bit from the conference table and leaned his elbows on his knees and folded his hands. "My dad served in WWII as a glider pilot, one of those 'Silent Wings' guys who flew into enemy territory. On a mission his plane crashed. Six weeks later he woke up in an Italian hospital. My dad said he had absolutely no memory of what had happened in those six weeks. He wanted to know. The Army said they had no information to share with him. He never believed that line."

"And he wanted you to use your skills as a reporter to try to piece together the lost weeks of his life?"

"Yeah, he desperately wanted to know what happened in those weeks. He thought I could just type in a few questions on the Internet and come up the answers. I told him the Internet doesn't hold the secrets of the universe." He looked up at me, "He made me promise to try. I never got around to it. I always thought I had plenty of time."

"When did your father die?"

"Two years ago last summer."

"So, for two years you've been holding onto your regret?"

"Yes, I can't seem to find a way to forgive myself."

"What sort of things do you say to yourself?"

"I tell myself I missed an opportunity to make my dad proud of me. I tell myself I was selfish to not have made time to help him find the answers he was looking for." He looked at his shoes, "I tell myself that I don't deserve to feel any peace and I'll have to live with regret for the rest of my life."

"Those are pretty harsh statements."

"Well," he said, "that's how I feel."

"If you had a friend who had the same situation what would you say to him?"

"Huh?"

"If you were in a position to give comfort to a friend in a similar situation, what would you say?"

"Well, I would say," he hesitated, "I would say, 'Don't be so hard on yourself. Everybody makes mistakes.'"

"Has anyone told you that?"

"Yes, my wife tried that," he chuckled.

"But you couldn't accept her compassion?"

"No, then she told me to talk to my mother."

"And did you?"

"Yes. My mom told me it wasn't too late to write Dad's story, if I really wanted to. She said his love for me wasn't tied to some old war story. She said Dad would be pleased whenever and if ever his story was told."

"Your mother must be a woman of faith."

"Oh, yes, she is. She believes Dad's in Heaven watching over all of us."

"And Heaven is a place where all hurts are healed," I said.

"You and my mom must go to the same church," he smiled slightly.

"It's never too late to keep a promise. I believe word gets around," I glanced up at the ceiling and smiled, "even to the most unlikely places."

"But what if I don't believe Dad could ever know I wrote his story?"

"Then I believe it would be enough for you to know you kept your promise."

Eric cleared his throat and quickly left the room.

In a few minutes Eric returned to the table. "I think I would like to try to write something to honor my dad."

"Okay. Let's see if there's a way we can lift off the guilt and open some new possibilities. In the workshop you said you wanted to write a novel about your dad's life. A novel is fiction. Do you want to make up the story or do you want to tell what really happened?" I asked.

"I want to tell what really happened," he said.

"Okay, then this is a big assignment. As a newspaper man accustomed to writing shorter pieces, would you be willing to lower the bar a little just to help you get started?"

"I'll do anything to get started."

"Choosing to write a short story or a family memoir about your dad's life would fulfill your promise, wouldn't it?"

"Yes, now that I think about it; that could work. Dad didn't really specifically say he wanted me to write a book about his life, he just wanted me to tell his story. Mainly he wanted me to find out about those lost six weeks."

"Your dad's story written as a family memoir would be a nice gift from your dad through you. It wouldn't have to be hundreds of pages long. You could make copies of your story and give them to family members at Christmas. How does that sound?"

"Less stressful," Eric was beginning to look hopeful, "And very doable."

I pulled out a piece of paper from my purse and wrote "Memoir" at the top of the sheet. "The family memoir format could be done in a few short chapters, kind of like a series of several newspaper articles. That way of writing is easy for you and would be a way to fulfill your promise to your dad too."

"But I still want to know about the missing six weeks," Eric said.

"I do too," I said as I wrote "Six weeks" with a big question mark beside it. I pointed to the question mark, "Have you done any research yet?"

"A little and what I uncovered is significant, but not helpful. The hospital in Italy burned to the ground about forty years ago. There are no records."

"Hmmm, no records could be a good thing."

"How can I tell a story without the facts?"

"Eric, your newspaper training is showing." He smiled.

"You have some facts, just not the facts you were hoping to find. The mystery stands. Does this open up a new possibility in your writer's mind?"

"Give me a hint?"

"Creative writing vs. newspaper writing, you know, historical fiction and creative non-fiction, Margaret Atwood did it with her book *Alias Grace*. Atwood found some old newspaper notice of a murder. If I remember the story right, the maid killed her employer. Atwood tracked down as many facts as she could and made up the rest. She creatively filled in the blanks. It was a fascinating book. You could do the same."

"But if I did that, it wouldn't be my dad's story."

"Well, not exactly, but your dad's story is a great story! It has all the right elements: a mysteriously lost six week time period, a main character you know very well, glider pilots, WWII, and of course, the possibility of a hidden romance! A fictionalized story of your dad's adventure could open you up creatively." I paused and wrote "Two stories" on the sheet, "Write two stories—the factual story to fulfill your promise and the fictionalized story just for fun."

Eric seemed to be getting interested.

"Where would I start?"

"Start with the plane crash and end it when your dad wakes up in the hospital."

"You mean make up the whole thing?!"

"Yeah, people do it all the time. It's called fiction."

A light appeared in Eric's eyes. I think he found a path to redemption.

Don't Let Your Emotions Run Away With Your Creative Life

The topic for the evening was printed in capital letters on the board: GOALS AND EMOTIONS.

"The last time we met each of you declared a creative goal and tried to think of three action steps to reach that goal. Would someone share their goal and get us started?" I asked.

Marc volunteered. "I want to learn a jazz repertoire." I wrote "repertoire" on the board.

"Why does this matter to you?" I asked.

"Until the basic tunes are set in my mind, I can't improvise."

"So what you're saying is you want to learn these tunes so you can become a better musician?"

"No, not really, I want to make music with my friends."

"Okay, so the payoff for learning the repertoire is more about friendship and fun than musical expertise?"

"Yes. I need to know the tunes so I can play in my friend's band."

Under "repertoire" I wrote "fun" and "time with friends."

"Marc, is this repertoire a large number of pieces?

"About fifty."

The class made a collective groaning sound.

"We think that sounds like a lot of work. Is this amount of work doable?"

"Oh yeah. It's possible. It'll take a long time though."

"Have you started on it?"

"Uh, no."

"What's keeping you from starting?"

"Learning fifty pieces feels overwhelming. I haven't really even thought about how to start."

"Does the intensity of that overwhelming feeling outweigh the feeling of fun you think you'd have playing in the band with your friends?"

"I'll have to think about that." Marc was beginning to see the connection between goals and emotions.

If I could have had some coaching time with Marc I would've asked him to tell me about his emotional connections with playing in the band. I would like him to tell me what it feels like to spend an evening playing guitar with his friends and how it feels to have an audience applaud after a song? Why does he enjoy spending time with his friends? While Marc answered my questions I would listen to his voice inflection and I would watch his body language. After Marc stopped talking I would ask him to tell me how he felt.

Sometimes we forget the things that really matter to us. We forget how happiness feels. As adults we spend so much of our time solving problems, we forget how much fun it is to enjoy life. Marc had forgotten, but when he remembers, he'll unpack that guitar.

How we think creates an emotional response—not the other way around. We don't feel an emotion first and then decide what we think about a situation. We think about the situation first, then our feelings emerge from our thinking.

The positive thinking statement is true: "Change your thinking, change your life." Thinking leads to emotions, emotions lead to action or inaction. Focus on what you want. Feel the good feelings tied to that accomplishment. Visualize the life you want to live. Keep that image firmly planted in your consciousness.

How Marc chooses to think about learning fifty pieces of music will determine his feelings about the task. How he feels will determine when and if he will ever begin practicing. Nailing the fifty pieces will net Marc what he's looking for—fun and friendship. If Marc focuses on the benefit of practicing instead of the work, he would be more likely to start practicing instead of just thinking about it or talking about it.

So long as Marc chooses to feel overwhelmed, he won't pick up his guitar. It's the feeling of being overwhelmed that's keeping Marc on the sidelines of the band—not the work of the repertoire. Marc admitted he could learn fifty songs—over time. Once he reframes his thinking to focus on the good feeling waiting for him, he won't have any trouble practicing.

Short-term   pain   nets   long-term   pleasure.   Delaying gratification is a common dilemma. We all have a hard time working today for a possible reward tomorrow. There's an emotional benefit in reaching a goal. There's an emotional cost in not reaching the goal. One feels good, the other feels bad.

"Anybody else?"

An older woman named Ruth spoke up, "I need to finish cleaning out my late mother's home." I wrote "Unfinished family business" on the board.

"Why is this important to you?"

"So I can put it on the market." I put a dollar sign beneath her goal.

"I'm curious. How long ago did your mother die?"

"Two years."

I noticed a couple of the younger adults in the room looked incredulous. Middle-aged adults with elderly parents are very aware of how much stuff can be crammed into a house!

"It's especially difficult to sort through someone's belongings when emotions run high," I said.

"At first I did grieve a little every time I opened a box of her stuff, but that passed after about a year. Now I'm beginning to resent the job. Dealing with her stuff keeps me from living my own life." Ruth was interested in scrapbooking and recording family stories. Her next statement was loaded with emotion. "Every day I feel as if I have to do her housework."

I wrote "time" under Ruth's dollar sign and "personal freedom." Resentment is a powerful negative emotion. It eats up your energy. Understandably, Ruth wanted to spend her retirement doing what she wanted to do—not cleaning up the mess her mother left behind.

"How does having the responsibility of all that stuff make you feel?" I asked.

"It makes me tired, mentally, emotionally and physically. I work on the stacks but I can't see any real progress. I go round and round trying to make decisions about what to keep and what to donate or trash."

"Have you ever daydreamed about how it will feel when the house is empty and sold?"

She leaned back in her chair, closed her eyes and let out a big exhale. "Oh yes, it will be wonderful! I can get back to my own life." Ruth had a very clear picture of life after the estate was settled. Seeing a future without her mother's stuff gave her a good feeling.

At break time, I talked to Ruth. It was clear to both of us that this job was too taxing to do alone. I encouraged her to limit the days per week she did "her mother's housework." If she could approach this task like a part-time job with set hours and days to work she could lessen her feelings of resentment. Being in charge of her time would make her feel more in charge of her own life. I encouraged her to hire someone to help her. Having someone to talk to while you do a hard task can make the task easier. A teenager in the neighborhood could be hired for minimum wage to pack boxes, fill sacks for recycling and make phone calls for donation pick-ups.

After the break Greg shared his creative goal. He wanted to write a murder mystery set in Iraq. He had a background in police work and Greg was a veteran. I could only imagine the interesting stories he could tell.

"Greg, why does it matter that you write?"

"I've got stories from the war swirling in my head all the time," he said almost desperately, "I need to get them out."

I wrote "novel" as Greg's goal and beneath it, I wrote "emotional release."

Kimberly said, "My goal is similar to Ruth's. I've got a clutter problem, except the junk is mine."

"Why is it important to you to get rid of your clutter?"

"Well, my junk is in two houses in two different cities." All the members of the class turned to look at Kim.

I asked the big question: "How does something like that happen?"

"Marriage, combining two households, divorce, getting the house in the divorce."

I wrote "simplify life" on the board. "Is this your goal?"

"That's exactly what I need."

"Why does simplifying your life matter?

"Two mortgages, time on the road. I've got a two-hour round trip each day." I drew another dollar sign on the board.

"If you could clear out one house and sell it, could you cut your expenses enough to have only one job?"

Kim nodded yes.

I wrote "time" under Kim's dollar sign. Before I turned from the board Kim spoke.

"There's one more reason why I need to simply my life," she spoke very quietly. I turned to look at her and the class gave her their full attention sensing something important. "My clutter isolates me from people. I'm embarrassed to have friends come over to my house. It's too full of junk." She hesitated, "I recently had a relationship end over my junk." She looked down and swallowed hard. "He said he just couldn't handle my stuff." Several of the women in the room winced at her honesty. After she spoke her truth, Kim looked like she had been to confession. Kim was broke, tired and lonely. There were plenty of negative emotions stealing the joy from her life.

I drew a heart next to Kim's "Time."

Brianna spoke up. "I want to paint again." Thankful for the shift in the discussion away from the pain of lost love, I wrote "paint" on the board.

"I put my painting career on hold while I was raising my teenagers. The last son was especially trying—actually he still is very trying. Dealing with him during his high school years took all my emotional energy." Brianna continued, "He just drained me. He's finally going to college in the fall."

"Out of town we hope?"

"Yes!"

The parents of teenagers cheered.

"Brianna, we understand why parenting trumped painting for some years, but why does painting matter enough now for you to declare it as your goal?"

"Painting makes me feel like an individual again, it's what I do for me. It's who I am. I am an artist." She thought for a moment, straightened her shoulders and said "And, painting is *fun*." I drew a happy face under the word "paint." I was familiar with Brianna's oil paintings of animals. Lots of color and thick paint. Lots of sales too.

I addressed the group. "Look at the board. The payoffs for reaching your goal are tangible. Some of you will realize an emotional payoff like Kim and Greg. Brianna and Marc will gain more fun in their lives. Kim and Ruth will realize financial gains and time to call their own. Once you identify your goal and understand why reaching your goal matters, you can also feel the positive emotions linked to reaching your goal. That's when you're ready to take action.

I asked the students to call out their action steps.

"Practice." (Marc)

"Paint." (Brianna)

"Go to the library to do research." (Greg)

"Call a teenager, friend and an antique dealer." (Ruth)

"Call a realtor." (Kim)

"Reclaim my studio space." (Brianna)

"Order a dumpster!" (Ruth)

"Order *two* dumpsters!" (Kimberly)

I added my own action step, "Write."

Work Better Under Pressure

The following email is one I received from a reader of *Art Focus Oklahoma Magazine*. This writer's question raises the problem of an absence of personal structure.

Dear Romney,

I have a job I enjoy and time in the evening to pursue my creative interests. I have story ideas swirling in my brain, but I rarely go to my office to write. It seems like my creativity and productivity went out the window when I graduated from college. What's going on with me?

My reply:

Dear Writer,

You're experiencing the post-college slump. First know this; the complacency you feel regarding your creative work may be due to a lack of structure in your life not a lack of moral fiber or diminishing talent. Many people once firmly placed in the world of work or marriage and family or both, devote less time to their creative work, resulting in products far below what had been produced for grades. This is distressing but not terminal. Your sagging creativity and inability to act on your creative ideas may be due to a lack of structure. You said you felt more creative and productive when you were in college. A lot of people share your opinion.

The structure of school provided these five important elements of success creative people need:

1.   Assignments
2.   Accountability
3.   Regular meeting times
4.   Support from peers
5.   A time to stop working!

Without these elements in place, many of us perform at lower levels of productivity. Here's why:

1. **Assignments:** As products of academic institutions, students learn quickly how to meet deadlines. Semester projects are assigned and due dates set. Our professors trusted we would be able to comply. If we got behind on projects, all it took was an all-nighter or two to insure our work would be completed by class time. While wrapped in the structure of high school, college or university, most students rose to the occasion and met the requirements to graduate, and those that could not, dropped out.

2. **Accountability**: The regimen of school also provided you with another important element that ensured your success—professors, advisors and mentors. Remember when a paper was returned to you, you hoped for more than a letter grade—you wanted a personal comment. An occasional positive word given by one we admire and want to emulate encouraged us to work harder and achieve more. College advisors kept us on track with our degree plan and counseled us through a variety of personal challenges.

3. **Regular meeting times**: Credit and non-credit classes have set meeting times. Attendance one or two times a week developed a habit over the semester. When we take a class we temporarily rearrange our personal and work lives around those class times. If you had an interesting professor, you'd look forward to the lecture. If your professor were less than stellar you'd still pleasantly anticipate the chance to see your friends and relish the time set aside from regular work and family responsibilities to simply think about your craft. Over time, your brain began to anticipate the next class meeting as a time when something pleasant could happen.

4. **Support from peers**: As an art student in college, the art building was my home. Even on weekends, art students would come and go, taking a couple of hours to paint or sculpt and visit with other students. It was a place of camaraderie. Without the presence of professors' critical eyes, we coached each other and offered tips on color or

composition. Students in a similar degree plan unknowingly build their own support group. Our college became community and family. When we left college, we also left behind our support group.

Fast forward from one generation to the next, my son experienced this same dilemma. After graduation from college, it didn't take long for Hunter to miss his friends, mentor professors and the art building. Without access to a building full of studio space, tools, easels and presses, he had to change the way he painted. Most of all he missed the conversation of like-minded creative peers. Working alone is just not as much fun.

5.   **A time to stop working!** When the pressure is on to complete a project or manuscript by deadline, you don't have time to be a perfectionist. At some point—usually minutes before the deadline—you simply had to let it go and quit. Once you ran out of time, you were forced to be satisfied with a "good enough" product. The structure of school gave us the "stop" button. Remember the relief you felt when you finally turned in a big project? You could stop worrying about it and get on with your life. Without the structure of school many creative people don't know how to "say when" and stop. Overworked paintings and too heavily edited manuscripts are the results of not having a real, enforced *deadline*.

Here are some tips on how you can reinsert a little structure back into your creative life:

1.   **Assignment**s: If you respond to assignments, enroll in a class. Professors of credit and non-credit classes expect their students to produce. Pay your tuition, buy your supplies and get back in the habit of meeting deadlines.

Outside of academia you can participate in juried art shows and writing contests—all with the much-needed hard and fast deadlines for entries. Look in the back of your professional magazines for these opportunities. I recommend *Art Calendar Magazine* for artists and *Byline* for writers.

2. **Accountability:** Enrolling in a class will give you the ear of your professor. Make an appointment during their office hours to discuss your work. Adjunct professors without offices and posted hours may be willing to talk with you before or after class to answer your questions. Your tuition in a community college or university setting includes many benefits including the services of professors, counselors, health services and employment advisors. Take advantage of these perks, you paid for them!

    If you choose not to take a class you can still build in accountability. Solicit a trusted friend with similar creative interests to meet with you for dinner a couple of times a month. Make a covenant to be ready every time to share your latest creative work. Read your manuscript. Show your painting in progress. Pretend you're paying for this privilege and you'll arrive prepared.

3. **Regular meeting time***s*: Get into the habit of attending annual workshops, conferences or retreats. Over time you'll begin to get to know people and you'll look forward to seeing them again. Your creative friends will ask "What have you been doing lately?" You'll want to have something exciting to report.

    Attending club meetings also provides this same opportunity for gathering and regular sharing. My writing group, Tulsa NightWriters, has a time at each meeting for brags. I like to have something to say!

4. **Support from peers**: If you're a people person, you may enjoy a support group. Some arts communities offer regular meeting times for creative people to gather. Artists meet at bookstores or coffee shops to discuss local marketing opportunities. Some groups of creative people have book clubs to work through a book one chapter at a time. A good book for a group of artists or writers might be Julia Cameron's *The Artist's Way.* Groups like this will require a leader, promoter and organizer. Check with your

local bookstore or church for a quiet space to meet. Some restaurants will also give you meeting space if your group eats lunch or dinner at the restaurant. Starting a group takes work but many will reap the benefits of meeting regularly with creative peers.

5.   **A time to stop working!** Exhibits and writing contests have real deadlines. One day late is too late. To retrain yourself to meet deadlines, make yourself stop even if your end product is only "good enough" in your opinion. Go ahead and enter it.

In school you didn't have the luxury of unlimited time to think too long about your ideas. Due to time restraints you had to choose an idea quickly and run with it.

Without real deadlines, many creative people think their ideas to death. With enough time any good idea can be killed by too much critical thinking. If you have unlimited time to think through all the possible shortcomings of an idea you may decide it is not artistically "important" enough to pursue and so you abandon it. You may think your idea is not original enough to be marketable and you toss the idea aside and continue your search for a more "exceptional" idea.

Spending all your work time culling ideas will keep you from producing anything. Be aware of what's going on inside your mind. You can't be critical and creative at the same time. Allow your creative ideas to flow while the idea is fresh—enjoy it. Don't be so quick to edit away your creativity.

To make yourself produce more, decide on a certain number of contests to enter each calendar year. Enter your work regularly and you'll improve your productivity. Call your alma mater and ask to schedule an art show in the gallery. The English department might welcome a guest author to talk with students about the work of a writer. Put something on the calendar and you'll work toward it. Reward your efforts after meeting a self-inflicted deadline by buying a book or special piece of art equipment. You can hit your reset button by putting your creative self on the line.

If you're reluctant to push yourself to this extent you may be one of those creative people who say they "work better under pressure." I question whether this idea is valid. These risk takers are hoping some bit of magic will descend from on high and save them from shame. Sometimes the Muse of creativity will save us, other times we flounder and fail and become discouraged. Many people who profess to be able to work better under pressure are more often than not caught in the grip of procrastination or perfectionism. It's best to lower the pressure and work a little every day. Steady work gives your right brain time to process new ideas and form them into new creative configurations. Let your ideas soak.

Looking back on my thirty years of formal education, I realize my professors taught me many things about the technical aspects of my craft but they did not teach me the psychology of being an artist or theologian. I was an "A" student, trained to work best under the structure and tutelage of academia. Upon graduation, I didn't even know what I didn't know! I definitely didn't know how to balance life and work to achieve measurable results. As an artist I floundered, unsure of the next right step to launch my career and unable to determine why I wasn't as successful as I had imagined I would be. This is why I welcome opportunities to speak to students. I want to introduce them to the psychological and practical skills they need to set and achieve their creative goals.

For a quick introduction to the inner work of the creative person, I recommend *The War of Art: Break Through the Blocks and Win Your Inner Creative Battles* by Steven Pressfield. Art and writing are mental games. We must know our inner opponent's tricks in order to win!

King Arthur's Round Table

Kelly's dream was to publish a book on nutrition, exercise and body image for teenage girls. Kelly was in her thirties, slim, athletic and dressed in a black t-shirt and jeans. Physically, she looked the part of a role model for young women, but today there was one thing was missing—serenity. Kelly was agitated and full of nervous energy, resentful and angry about something.

She began, "I've wanted to do this book for over ten years." She raised her voice, "Ten years!" Kelly had a stinging awareness of lost time.

"My first book was rejected. The publisher said the exercise illustrations looked stiff and the photos were boring."

"Did you get your artist to re-do the drawings?"

"My cousin told me he would re-do the illustrations. He's a commercial artist, but he hasn't gotten around to helping me." She sat back in her chair and crossed her arms.

"Does your cousin live nearby?"

"Yes, right here in town."

"You get along?"

She curled her hands in fists and knocked them together—twice, "We butt heads."

"That doesn't sound promising. Do you know of another person who could do the drawings?" I asked.

"I met an artist at a conference last year. She did the exercise illustrations for a yoga magazine. She seemed interested in my idea," Kelly thought for a split second, "but my cousin will do the work for free."

"But he's not doing it."

Kelly looked at me as if I had insulted her family.

With measured words I stated a fact. "If it's important enough to you to do this project, call this artist and ask her to quote you a price for the work."

Kelly didn't comment. She jumped into her next story.

"My friend was supposed to help me shoot the still photos. He does graduation portraits. He said he could round up some models."

I was afraid I knew what was coming.

"He hasn't had time to help me either. He says his family and business take up all his time." She threw up her hands high in the air and let them drop in her lap.

"Was the photographer going to do the work for free too?"

"Yes, he's an old college friend."

"But his hands are full."

"Everybody's too busy to help me." She sighed.

"I know," I said.

She drooped back into the comfort of the chair. "I don't know what to do."

"You pay a plumber when you need one?" I asked the question with a little smile, already knowing her answer.

"Well, yes."

She gave me a slight, quizzical frown, as if to say, "What's that got to do with me?" and I felt my smile broaden.

"So hire professionals to do what you can't do. That's part of the cost of doing business. If people are getting paid, they usually find the time to do the work. There's another plus too, if you don't like their work you can fire them. It's harder to fire your cousin or your friend."

"Yes, but I don't want to pay to have this work done if they're going to tell me it's not good enough."

A "Yes, but" response is a sure sign that person isn't listening.

For the time being Kelly wasn't willing to assume the responsibility to create, protect and fulfill her own dream. She wanted to believe her problems were caused by other people and should be solved by other people. The list of people who were keeping her down got longer by the minute—first her cousin, then her friend, now "they."

I said nothing, just watched her deal with the uncomfortable silence. She tried again, "But what if they tell me something else is wrong with the book?"

"Don't you want to know if something needs to be fixed? At least they're taking the time to make a suggestion. Do whatever the publisher tells you to do. Say 'Thank you for your suggestion and your time,' and then get the corrections made a.s.a.p. and send it back."

She folded her arms again and sighed. She looked as if I wasn't telling her what she wanted to hear. I tried to shift the conversation.

"Tell me about your market research?"

"What do you mean?"

"Have you looked at your competition?"

"Oh, yeah. Denise Austin's got all kinds of exercise stuff out there. Just Google her name! I get jealous and mad when I see *her* marketing machine."

Denise Austin just hit the list after "they."

"What I mean is have you analyzed the exercise book market? Is anyone else writing specifically for teenage girls about exercise and body image?"

"I don't know. There are books on exercise and body image for adult women but I can't think of any book specifically for the teenage market."

"Have you checked out the magazines young girls read? What kinds of articles do they run on fitness and body image?" I asked.

"I don't know." She gave me an exasperated look. I was reminded of a time when my son called with a list of complaints about his college roommate. I asked him if he wanted to brainstorm or if he just wanted to vent. He was honest and told me he needed to vent. After about ten minutes he was ready to do some problem solving.

Kelly continued, "I'm trying to write a book. I don't have time to read magazines!"

I felt Kelly had just written my name on her "list" directly after Denise Austin.

"Market research pays off. Find out what's selling. A non-fiction book is a lot like a long magazine article."

I continued to coach Kelly through the process of analyzing the market. Writers serious about writing need to know what's selling. They read books and magazines on their craft, go to workshops and analyze the work of other writers. They seek out advice from people who know the ropes and take that advice—all that in addition to writing.

Artists serious about selling not only master technique but they visit galleries, read magazines and books on the business of art, attend workshops, develop a networking base, and they paint. The business of art is a business.

In our conversation Kelly told me she'd put some effort in on her first try to get published but not a lot. She admitted she hoped she'd get lucky, when she didn't, she got frustrated and quit. The world went on without her. Nobody missed her book.

"From what you've told me the editors didn't have a problem with your text. That's important to remember. You've done the biggest part of the work." I tried to encourage her.

"Thanks. I do feel good about my writing."

"What you still need is new illustrations and photos. Kelly, do you feel this project too big to do alone?"

"That's what I've been telling you. I need help!"

"Kelly, you need a carefully chosen team. Trying to get a book published and marketed is hard work. Do you remember the story of King Arthur and the Knights of the Round Table?"

"Camelot?"

"Yes. You need some King Arthur Roundtable basics."

I took a piece of paper and drew a circle. "This is your round table." I drew a cartoon king sitting at the head of the table in a fancy "king" chair with armrests.

She seemed interested.

"You are King Arthur."

She looked up at me, "And that means?"

"King Arthur surrounded himself with knights who could help him achieve his goals for Camelot. Camelot was Arthur's priority, his goal."

I drew some empty chairs around the table.

"The round table was a symbol for Arthur's dreams for Camelot. His dream was too big to do by himself. Arthur chose each knight for what he could bring "to the table." I tapped my finger on the drawing of the round table. "On this table is your project." I tapped at the king, "You are the king."

She held her forehead with elbows propped on her knees. I couldn't decide whether Kelly was overwhelmed or confused.

"You could identify the knights you need to help you achieve your goal, your Camelot. Who do you need at your round table?"

"Well, a photographer."

I scribbled "photographer" above one of the sketched chairs.

"An artist." I wrote "artist" above another chair.

"Yes, and she's already expressed some interest in your idea. She just needs to be contacted. If you're thinking about an accompanying video you'll need music too."

"Yeah. I need somebody to write some original music or help me sort through the copyright laws about royalties. I don't have any idea about that stuff."

"You could hire somebody to investigate that for you," I added.

I drew a treble clef above another chair.

I could see Kelly was finally beginning to engage in the process.

"Okay, tell me about your money? Do you have some financing for this project or ready cash?"

"I have a backer. He's just waiting for me to get it done."

"That's great! Maybe he can advance you some money to pay for the work you need to get done right away." I drew a dollar sign above another chair at Kelly's roundtable.

"Maybe." Her tone of voice had just shifted to a whine. "But what if I work really hard and they tell me it's not good enough?"

She'd circled right back to where we'd started.

"Kelly, are you or "they" in charge of your life?"

Her eyes flashed with anger. "You don't understand. I just don't want to be disappointed again."

"Nobody likes to be disappointed. No question about it, what you're trying to do is big, and there could be some big pay-offs for your efforts too."

I redirected her attention to my drawing of the king. I wrote "King Kelly" above the crown.

"This is your dream. You're the only one who cares enough to make it happen." I paused while she studied the roundtable notes, "Sit in the king's chair and make your dream a reality or walk away from the table."

She put her head in her hands and sighed. I waited.

She sat up and straightened her shoulders. She looked capable and confident. "Okay. I'll take the chair. I don't want to waste any more time." Kelly looked ready to go to work.

A roundtable is one way to solicit help from other professionals for an important project. Be willing to partner with other people to make your dreams a reality.

King Arthur's Roundtable Basics

1. State your goal. What's on the table?
2. Accept your responsibility to be in charge. Be the King.
3. Make a list of all the tasks that must be done in order to reach your goal.
4. Brainstorm possible leaders for each of these tasks.
5. Ask people to be on your team who are emotionally or financially invested in your dream. Your knights may be friends, family members or hired contractors. State with clarity and conviction the reasons why their skills are essential to your success.

6.   Set a date for a first meeting with your team whether all your "knights" are in place or not.

7.   Ask the group to help you outline the sequence of tasks that must be done. Set a deadline for each task.

8.   Value the time of each team member. Decide how often to meet. Each meeting should last an hour or less.

9.   Regularly express appreciation to your team members.

10.   Celebrate the completion of your project.

Each member of your roundtable will feel valued when asked to bring their best gifts to the table. A roundtable team of advisors will keep you focused, positive and accountable to your deadlines. If you're not operating in real time, it's easy to postpone action and nothing happens. Kelly desperately needed a deadline. In our coaching session, she set several deadlines and expanded her list of "knights."

At some time or another most of us will need the input and counsel of others to make our dreams a reality. Kelly's frustration level lifted and she shifted into action when she admitted she didn't have the experience or expertise to do all the tasks alone. She needed help from others and she needed the support and accountability of a team. When Kelly decided to be strategic and make a financial investment in her dream, she started to believe it was possible.

Don't Leave Your Creativity at Home

It's not uncommon for creative people to blame their day jobs for their lack of creative output. In my classes and in coaching sessions I hear all kinds of plausible reasons for why people aren't using their creative gifts in their off hours. One teacher said, "If only I didn't have to teach special education students all day I could work on my one-woman stage show in the evening. Every day when I finally get home, I'm too tired to be creative." A man in one of my classes complained about his own business practices when he told me: "If only I didn't have to do so much watch repair work I could work on my own jewelry designs."

"If only" statements sound reasonable but they're really excuses. A day job is what it is—a source of income that requires a limited number of hours each day. Your job may take the most productive hours of your day but that doesn't mean you have to surrender all your waking hours to your job and give every ounce of your creativity to the boss. After you leave work your creative projects deserve a part of your available time.

Lots of creative people successfully juggle two or more jobs. Having more than one income stream is a plus. Fine artists sell their watercolors and teach art lessons to adults. Dancers in professional dance companies teach ballet to children in after-school classes and summer camps. Professional musicians play in orchestras and teach private lessons. Novelists teach writing courses at community colleges.

Maybe your day job is in a totally unrelated field. You can be a special education teacher and an actor. You can be an artist and a motivational speaker. You can write technical manuals for the government and the Great American Novel—all at the same time. A job in a field unrelated to your passion may actually be a plus. Having a full or part-time job that doesn't tap your creative energies is a good thing! A job in an unrelated field frees your brain to do creative thinking and problem solving.

My oldest son, Hunter, writes spoken word poetry. He worked as a waiter at a very trendy downtown restaurant. On breaks he occasionally performed his poetry to the dinner guests. One night last summer the dishwasher didn't show for his shift and the owner asked him to fill in for the dishwasher. Hunter washed dishes all evening and enjoyed it. He said there was something meditative and soothing about the hot water and the suds and a feeling of accomplishment with every action—dishes come in dirty and go out clean.

He said, "Here's the best part of being a dishwasher. I don't have to schmooze with the customers to try to get tips. I can simply do my job. My brain is free to think. When a phrase surfaces I dry my hands and capture it in a notebook I keep in my apron pocket. I can practice my act while I wash dishes. Nobody cares if I talk to myself while I work." He shrugged his shoulders. "I'm probably the only college graduate dishwasher in town. I like washing dishes. It frees my brain for more important things."

Thinking about your creative work while you're at work is energizing. Keep a notebook beside your workspace and record your thoughts during the day. Your new ideas will call you to action in your off hours. With some preplanning you can build in some time for your creative work during your workday.

Here are ten suggestions:

1. If you're an early riser, arrive at work a half-hour earlier than required. Write, sketch or work on your beading project at your desk.

2. If your commute is slow due to rush hour traffic consider staying at work a half-hour later. Use this time to work on your creative project. The office is quiet and you'll avoid the rush hour stress by waiting a while before leaving the office. Use the time to mentally leave your office cares and worries at the office. Visualize the time you'll spend in the evening continuing your creative activities.

3. At break time, use your ten or fifteen minutes to read a book or magazine article about some aspect of your creative field. Imagine how much knowledge you could gain by reading one article a day from *Writer's Digest* or

Art in America! Pull out that stack of magazines you've been intending to read and take them to work.

If your free time at work is very limited, choose something easy to read. I suggest Strunk and White's *The Elements of Style,* Robert Henri's *The Art Spirit* or *The War of Art* by Steven Pressfield. Think of it in this way, smokers leave the office for several nicotine hits during the workday; you're taking a creativity break!

4. Use your lunch hour to work on your writing or sketch at your desk. Pack a lunch two or three times a week instead of going out with your co-workers. You'll save money (for extra paint or more books!) and you can add in at least half an hour of writing time into your day.

5. Decorate your workplace with reminders of your creative goals. Display examples of your artwork. Post an inspiring poem. Put up a photograph of the vacation spot you'll visit when your book royalties begin. You are more than the job you perform, you are also who you are becoming.

6. Have an on-going list of the things you appreciate about your job. Gratitude raises your spirits. Your job provides income and benefits and also allows you evening and weekend free time to pursue your creative interests. The people with whom you work also become your support community, friends and patrons. Be thankful for your job.

7. Actively seek out ways your job can inform and enrich your creative life. Writers are always on the lookout for interesting story lines and characters; your workplace is full of real life dramas. Artists in the workplace are surrounded by possible models. Playwrights can find willing actors within your department at your day job. Your job can enrich your creative endeavors. Listen and watch for what is right before your eyes. Everything counts.

8. Spend your drive time listening to CD's and books on tape that address your creative interests. We all know that the monotony of driving often frees up creative thoughts. When a good idea surfaces I try to jot it down as soon as

possible rather than trying to remember it. This frees up my brain to continue its creative play. I keep a pencil and a thick spiral notebook in the front passenger seat of my car to record thoughts (the weight of the spiral keeps it in place on the car seat). Use your cell phone to call home and leave yourself a message regarding your writing or artwork. A sound activated hand-held recorder would be the easiest to use—that beautiful phrase of dialogue can be recorded so much more quickly and safely while driving. When you get home all your musings are ready to be added to your work in progress.

9.   Begin the night before. Before you go to bed, write down three goals for the next day. These goals should be related to your creative work such as: Order art supplies on my lunch hour or draw a timeline of my main character's childhood. If you give your brain an assignment, it will work on it while you're asleep and during the next day. When you wake up in the morning you'll know what you want to accomplish on short breaks from your routine.

10.   Create a screensaver that will remind you of your true vocation. Display prints of famous paintings or quotes from famous authors. These will inspire you throughout the day and help you remember your true vocation.

Don't leave your creativity at home when you go to work. With some planning it's easy to rearrange your workday to include small snippets of time for your real passion—your creative work. You'll feel less tired at the end of the day when you've added in time for your creative work.

Painting, clay work, beading, writing and practicing the piano energize our inner spirits making us less weary and more positive. You are an artist, practice your art and enjoy the mental and physical benefits.

Be honest about how you spend your evenings and weekends. Household chores and family responsibilities don't have to be given all our waking hours. Do you veg out in front of the TV watching reruns? Do you have your head in a novel looking for an escape? Haven't you already discovered that doing your creative work is the best escape of all?

The key is to actively make time during your day for what's important to you. Even twenty minutes a day for your own creative interests will increase your happiness. Your day job and home responsibilities can't keep you from any creative activity you sincerely want to pursue.

PART III:
Protecting Your Time and Talents

Approaching Elephants
Always Arrive on Time

"I want to know why people keep asking me to do stuff for free." Allison was agitated. The tell-tale signs of her ADHD were evident—her right leg bounced up and down. Allison and I met at Starbucks for coffee. Privately I thought she didn't need any extra caffeine.

"What kind of stuff are you being required to do?" I asked.

"Writing articles, writing text for websites; you know PR stuff. I'm tired of it."

"Why would someone ask you to work for free?" I asked Allison the same question she asked me.

She paused for a moment "Well, because," she drank a tiny sip of her cappuccino, "I've done work for free for these people before."

"You just answered your own question."

Allison looked a little surprised. "I guess that makes sense," she said.

"Yes, it makes perfect sense. Why would anyone offer to pay you when your pattern is to give your time and talents away? You can't fault them for asking. They're just doing what works most economically for them."

"Wow," she said as she shook her head side to side, "Is it that simple to understand?"

"Most of the time it is that logical. Do you want to change your pattern?" I asked.

"Yeah. What should I do?"

"Change expectations, but we'll talk about that in a minute. First tell me why you used to work for free."

"I like the way you said 'used to.'" Allison's shoulders dropped a degree or two. She was beginning to look a little less stressed. "Some years ago when I decided to become a freelance writer I didn't feel confident enough about my skills to charge for them, so I decided to volunteer my time to gain some writing experience."

"Volunteering is an excellent way to gain experience and make new contacts. Did you get what you needed from doing those free jobs?"

"Yes, I did."

"Do you think you gained the writing experience you needed within twelve months or so?" I asked.

"That's probably right, about a year or so."

"A minute ago you used the phrase 'some years ago.' That leads me to believe that you've been volunteering for a long time, am I right?"

She reluctantly agreed with my conclusion.

"For some reason you continued working as a volunteer past the time when you had gained the experience you wanted. What we have to figure out is why."

"At the time when I started doing freelance work for free, I felt I was moving toward my goal."

"And you were. I'm curious about something though," I gave her a moment to tune in, "When you agreed to enter into a relationship with that organization, did you have an idea in mind of how long you would continue your association with them? Did you have an exit strategy?"

"Exit strategy?" Allison looked a little confused. "I never gave any thought to how long I would stay."

"In volunteer agencies, officers may serve for a year or two. At the end of the term, people drop out or rotate to a new position. When other people rolled off the board, did it ever occur to you to do the same?"

Allison shook her head from side to side. "No, my job as freelance writer was not an actual position on the board. I did jobs as they came along. What should I have done instead?"

"You could have looked at volunteering in a more business-like way. When you decided to associate with this group you could've said to yourself 'My reason for signing on with this group is to get experience. I think I can get enough writing experience in six months to a year. At the six month mark I'll take time to evaluate this use of my time and make a decision to either stay or go.'"

"I've never thought that strategically about anything in my whole life." She placed her hands on her knees and leaned back away from the table.

"Think about it this way. If you had a clear reason to get in, which you did, then it would be reasonable to get out when your personal 'mission' was accomplished. Without an exit plan, without some sort of a time frame, you had no reason to leave and time rolled on."

"I never thought much about how much time I was spending doing volunteer work until lately," she admitted. "Somewhere along the way things got out of hand."

"Are there additional reasons why you stayed longer than you needed to?"

"I hoped writing for this group would get my name out there for other jobs."

"Did your name get around as a writer?" I asked.

"Yes, it did, in fact, it snowballed. I was flattered by the calls until I discovered most of the requests were from other non-profits wanting me to do the work for free."

"Your name got around all right, as a person who would work for free. That kind of press sabotaged your efforts to build a real business base," I said.

Allison nodded in agreement. "I kept thinking somebody would offer to pay me, but nobody ever brought up money."

"And you didn't ask to be paid?"

"No, by the time I had chatted with them for a while I felt obligated to agree to do a little job for them. You know someone says 'You come so highly recommended, blah, blah, blah.'"

"Flattery," I smiled at her. "You must bond quickly."

"I know. I'm a goner if I hear 'This job doesn't have to be done for six months, so don't feel any pressure, there's no rush.'"

"Whoa. That's an approaching elephant," I said.

"Who said anything about elephants?"

"An approaching elephant is a request for your time that has two main elements: the job doesn't have to be done right away, the deadline can be months out into the future and the second element is that you aren't really interested in the job. You didn't want to do it, but you agreed to do it anyway. You may have said 'Yes' to please somebody else or because you couldn't think of a nice way to say 'No.'"

"I can never think of a nice way to say 'No.'" Allison said. "That's how I get trapped."

"You allow yourself to get trapped. Instead of giving yourself time to consider all the ramifications of the job, you say 'Yes' too quickly."

"As soon as I said 'Yes,' I wished I'd said 'No.'"

"It's happened to me often enough too." I said. "It's a hard habit to break once people think they know what response to expect from you."

I got up from the table and walked over to the counter and picked up a stack of paper napkins. I took a pen out of my purse and drew a horizontal line in the middle of the napkin. Above the line I drew a hot swirling sun. On the horizontal line I drew a dark spot with the pen. I pointed to the spot. "Allison, this spot is an approaching elephant. He's way off in the distance, months away. He is no threat to you now because you are here," I drew an X at the bottom of the napkin. "You've agreed to do some job—for pay or for-free, it doesn't really matter. You think you've got plenty of time to do the job later, so you procrastinate. You know you really don't want to do the job, but you hope you might warm up to the idea eventually, but that doesn't happen either. You say to yourself 'Surely that little job won't take a lot of time. I'll do it later.' You don't do the job today or tomorrow or for several weeks. For some time that elephant stays way off in the distance. He's just a speck on the horizon line, but as the months pass the elephant walks toward you, one step at a time. After a while, you can feel him coming. Your anxiety and guilt grows with every step he takes."

I draw a shape of an elephant a little closer. "A month from the deadline the person who asked you to do the job makes a friendly check-in call, 'How's it going? Do you have any questions?' You lie and say you have everything under control, but when you look for your notes on the project, you can't find them. You begin to feel pushed and anxious. You may start to feel resentment toward that person and her organization. You avoid seeing that person. You check your caller I.D. and don't pick up when she calls. You don't return her emails. But all that avoidance does not make the elephant disappear. You look out your window and there's the silhouette of your personal elephant. He's clearly in view and getting bigger by the minute. He's slowly and surely coming closer and closer." I draw the elephant a bit bigger. Allison began to chuckle.

"The week before the job is due you finally dig out your paperwork and discover the job is bigger than you thought. Now you can't even be mad at the person who asked you to do the job, but you're plenty mad at yourself for not having the guts to say 'No' when you had the chance. You belittle yourself for not having any backbone. Three days before the job is due, you wake up and the elephant is no longer approaching. He's on your driveway. Now he's banging his trunk on your window demanding entrance! The approaching elephant has arrived right on time! Approaching elephants *always* arrive on time."

Allison laughed out loud. "What happens next?"

"In a panic, you call your creativity coach hoping she can give you an easy out." We both giggled.

"So what should I do?" she asked.

"In the future don't agree to any request without thinking about it for at least a couple of days. Stall. When you get one of those approaching elephant phone calls remember how uncomfortable it is to have an elephant at your house. Say 'Thanks for thinking of me. I'll have to check my calendar and get back to you.' Then go home and think about whether you want to do the job or not."

"I sure need to do that. Maybe I'd have fewer headaches," she said.

"Allison, If you had a crowded suffocating feeling when the person told you about the project, your body was desperately trying to convince you to say 'No.' If you're mildly interested, then you need to take some time to investigate the project further. Think about whether this project enhances your career goals or detracts you from them. Some projects are simply time-consuming detours. You are the only person who can decide whether this new request is an opportunity that fits your career goals, interests and available time."

"I'm so tired I want to say 'No' to everything from now on!"

"You can if you want to, but if you want to maintain a business you'll need to at least consider taking paying jobs, right?"

"Well, yes, I need the work."

"So devise a way to screen out the freebies from the paying jobs before you get too enmeshed with the caller. Say something like: 'I might want to submit a bid for your job. Do you have a budget for the work?' This lets the person know right up front that you expect to be paid."

"Oh, wow, that sounds good!"

"Write it down and put it by the phone so you can read it when you get the next call. If the person has a budget and you want to do the job, then submit a bid for the work. If you hear, 'We're a non-profit organization and don't have a budget.' You say, 'I understand. I did work for a lot of years for non-profits, but I no longer have the time to do any work on a volunteer basis.'"

"That makes me sound really successful!"

"You'll be more successful when you quit working for free!"

"But what if the job doesn't sound like anything I want to do—even for pay? What should I say?" Allison grabbed a napkin.

"Wait a minute. I need to write these phrases down before I forget them." She looked up, "What did you say again?"

"Thanks for thinking of me, but that job isn't a fit for me at this time." I waited while she copied the line on her napkin. You don't have to tell them why you're not interested or explain all you've learned about taking charge of your business life. Just decline."

"What's the line that screens the for-pay jobs?" she asked.

"I might want to submit a bid for your job. Do you have a budget for the work?" More scribbling.

"What was the polite one that gives me time to think it over?"

"Thanks for thinking of me. I'll have to check my calendar and get back to you."

Allison finished writing the phrases and stacked her napkins beside her empty coffee cup. She smiled as she placed the approaching elephant illustration on top of the stack.

"How do I get myself into these messes?" she asked absently.

"Have you got any ideas about that?"

She seemed surprised that I expected an answer. "Well, I know I'm a people pleaser," she said.

"People like to be liked," I said, "I think you're getting over that bad habit. It finally costs too much. Other ideas?"

"I also underestimate the length of time it will really take to complete a project. I've never gotten a handle on that. Even with my paying jobs I spend too much time doing them and end up losing money on the job."

"Creative people often underestimate the amount of time a job will take. We think our creative thinking skills make us smarter and faster than other people. We forget we also fight procrastination and perfectionism, these time wasters slow us down. It's not uncommon for creative people to undervalue their skills and talents and undercharge for their services."

"Or give them away for free," Allison said. She leaned across the table, "Let's get back to what I'm going to say the next time someone calls me to do a job for free. What do I say if the person pushes me to give them an answer?"

"Allison, here's your assertiveness training, say: 'If you need to know today, the answer is 'No.'"

"Oh, that's good!" She looked pleased. "Wait a minute. Let me write that one down too." She wrote on another napkin.

"Sometimes the person asking is just trying to get this item off of their list of things to do. You can understand that they probably have taken on too many responsibilities too. If you say 'No' they'll just call the next name on their list."

"Okay, these will help." Allison patted her stack of napkins. "Now what can I do about all the elephants that are headed my way?"

I pushed another paper napkin across the table towards her. "Make a list of the ones you can remember while I go get us some water. I love having coffee at Starbucks but I hate it that there are no friendly refills."

When I returned to the table Allison had a list of eight jobs written on a paper napkin. "Put the dates when these are due next to the job."

She dated her elephants. Three jobs were due in the next month. Two jobs were due in four months. Three were due in six to eight months.

"Are any of these jobs for pay?"

"No, I didn't list the paying jobs. I'll do those. These are the freebies."

I shook my head, "Have you put any time in on any of these jobs?"

"Only a little time on the ones due next month."

"Do you feel morally obligated to do the jobs due next month?"

"Yes. It's too late for me to not do them and feel okay about myself."

"Okay, then take care of these three. Would you be open to renegotiating the other elephants?"

"How do I do that?"

"Reset new expectations. You can change your mind, you know. Give the organization an opportunity to forge a new relationship with you as a freelancer, instead of a volunteer.

You've done good work for them for a long time. They know you're dependable. They might not want to break in a new person. Give them a chance to form a new alliance. Simply call to make an appointment to have additional conversation about the jobs."

"Oh, this is making me feel nervous," Allison said with a whine in her voice.

"No reason to be nervous. People renegotiate relationships all the time. It's a *business* practice. You could say 'I've enjoyed working with this organization as a volunteer writer, but now that my freelance business is taking off, I can't give my time away any more. Could I submit a bid for the job I was going to do as a volunteer?" If she or he hesitates add, 'Or for the next writing job that comes along?' At that point you might have an opportunity to talk about your hourly rate."

"What do I say if when she says they don't have a budget to pay for writing?" Allison seemed sure that this would be the case.

"Then you say 'I understand. I'm sure you'll be able to find someone who needs an opportunity to gain writing experience.'"

She grimaced. "Allison, you don't have to feel like you're leaving them in a lurch, there's a big window of time to find a replacement writer."

She looked a little less reluctant, "Okay, what do I say again?"

"Repeat after me: 'I understand. I'm sure you'll be able to find someone else to do the job, someone who needs this valuable experience.'"

Allison repeated the sentence.

"Say it with a period at the end of the sentence."

She tried again with a little more confident tone, and then she added, "Who knows, there may be somebody out there that really does need the experience!"

"Now you're talking! You're doing a favor for someone else," I said.

I felt like Allison and I had completed our coaching session. I picked up my purse as a signal that I thought we were finished.

Allison spoke, "But if I'm not willing to volunteer my time as a writer anymore, does that mean I have to leave the group? I've made lots of friends over the years. Do I have to drop out?"

"Who said anything about dropping out?" I asked.

Allison looked surprised. "Won't I have to quit being a part of this organization if I don't want to work for free?"

"Not necessarily. You can still be a volunteer if you want to; just don't do any more freelance writing for free. Ask for a new assignment that is less time consuming and doesn't involve writing in any way. You might like to co-chair a committee with one of your friends. You don't have to drop out just because you're changing the expectations of what they can expect you to do. You'll just have to be aware of your pattern and take care not to repeat it."

"I take charge of what happens next?" Allison asked.

"That's how to change expectations, decide what you want to happen and see if you can negotiate that. You're always in charge. If you want to change expectations, you have to be willing to do it yourself."

Allison picked up her purse and I picked up mine.

Unfortunately, many good-hearted creative people often give their time and talents away. Writers, artists, singers, and musicians are asked to donate their skills, services and products to charitable organizations, churches, schools, hospitals, political parties and causes of all types. Friends ask, your child's sports team asks, and teachers ask. You don't have to give your time and talents away—unless you want to.

Remember, an invitation to donate your time or skills is an invitation. You can say "No." A request for your talents is the same as a phone solicitor asking for a donation. You always have two choices: agree or decline.

To help you make a decision you must objectively appraise whether this opportunity fits your career goals. I offer the following key questions to help you make an informed decision when faced with a request for your time, energy or talents.

1.   Will this particular "opportunity" move me closer to or further away from my desired career goals?

2. Do I have enough of a special interest in helping this group that I'm willing to donate my time or services? This may be the case with your child's school or your church.
3. Do I have the time available to do this job by the due date without feeling pressure?
4. What are my motives? Am I agreeing to do the job to fulfill an obligation? Am I trying to get people to like me?
5. What is my gut feeling about this request?
6. Especially on a request for a donation of time or services, ask yourself, "Do I like the people I'll be working with enough to spend time with them?"
7. Is there anything new I can learn from doing this project?
8. Try to predict the future. Will this task rob me of my energies and cause me to feel resentful in the long run or do I think it will energize me?

As a coach, I want you to keep the big picture in mind: any "opportunity" that comes along will require some amount of time and energy on your part. No job is ever as easy as we hope it will be. Creative people are notorious for underestimating the time it will take to do a project and they often undercharge for their time. Do you know what the going rate is for your services in the marketplace?

Your time is valuable. Your skills have been honed over time through schooling, workshops, and years of work experience. What may seem easy for you may not be easy for everyone else to do—that's why you get the call. Your creative skills and talents deserve compensation. Allison hoped someone else would bring up the subject of money. That was her job to do. Don't rely on other people to advocate for your best interests. Only you can stick up for yourself. You're in charge of your career, your feelings and your future.

Be realistic, any task will take time. There may be phone calls, emails, conferences, preparation time, costs for materials that may or may not be reimbursed, mileage, postage, research time etc. Don't do whatever comes along and hope it will move your career forward. Be strategic! Choose the right opportunity at the right time for your career goals.

Be a Plate Spinner

I was the guest speaker for the monthly meeting of a regional writers group. Following the meeting two of the officers invited me to lunch at an Italian restaurant. The late summer temperature was in the high 90's making the cool, dark dining room especially pleasant. Small spotlights illuminated the walls decorated in gold, red, and black. It was a perfect place for quiet conversation and reflection. A slim young woman dressed in black brought menus to our table. She wore a blond ponytail styled in a messy twist.

Julia and Evelyn complemented me on the morning workshop before they asked about my coaching practice.

"Tell us what you *really* do." Evelyn said leaning across the table. Evelyn was a retired high school counselor.

"I listen and ask the next right question."

"How do you know what's the next right question?" Julia asked.

Julia and Evelyn looked hungrily curious, as if they were about to hear a piece of gossip.

"There's no *one* right question. It depends on the situation. And, of course, the situation is different every time."

Evelyn nudged Julia in the ribs, "Ask your question."

Julia shot her friend an aggravated look. Evelyn sat back in the booth and smiled smugly.

Julia cleared her throat, "This is the question we've been arguing about: How many times should a person rewrite a book before sending it to a publisher?"

"How many rewrites have you made on your book already?" I asked.

"Ha!" Evelyn squealed as she slapped her hands down on the tabletop. "She's onto you already!"

Julia closed her eyes and inhaled as if she could gather patience from the atmosphere. "Five or six times."

"Not hardly! Try about ten times! She won't let it go!" Evelyn spoke a little too loudly for restaurant protocol.

"Evelyn, that's not true! I'll let it go once I think it's good enough!"

"Like that will ever happen." Evelyn looked over her reading glasses at me with a knowing teacher-to-teacher look.

"I want it to be as perfect as it can be before I send it off. I don't want any typos or incomplete sentences." Julia explained.

"That's reasonable." I said. Julia looked pleased that I understood.

"But," Evelyn argued, "There's got to be some point where you call it quits and move on to the next project, isn't that right, Romney?"

"That's also true," I said. Both women had legitimate points. "It's important to have your writing as polished as possible and it's also important to be able to let it go and move on to a new project."

"Julia, tell Romney about your novel."

Julia shared the plot of her mystery. It sounded very promising.

"Tell me why Evelyn is so anxious for you to send it off."

The year before, Julia and Evelyn had attended a writing conference sponsored by a hot-shot independent publisher. Julia made an appointment with him and pitched her book. Julia told me with pride that he'd invited her to send in a couple of chapters. She mailed two chapters within the week.

"Tell her what happened next." Evelyn prodded.

"He asked to see the whole book." Julia said.

"How exciting! How long ago was this?" I asked.

"A little over a year."

"Is your book finished?"

"No, I haven't been able to finish it. I'm probably about three-quarters of the way through."

"What's keeping you from finishing your book?"

"I keep editing the opening chapters."

"I could edit the chapters for her if she would just let me see them." Evelyn said. "I'm a good editor. I used to teach composition classes, for God's sake."

"Julia, I'm a little confused, are you rewriting or doing line edits?" I asked. I needed to know exactly what she was doing.

"Rewriting."

Evelyn's eyebrows shot up in surprise. "Oh! Now it's even worse than I thought."

This lunch was turning into tag team coaching.

"Julia, are you rewriting the chapters the publisher said he liked?"

"Yes." She looked down.

"Doesn't that feel risky? You know, tampering with success?"

"Maybe it is, but I want it to be perfect!"

"Do you feel you're getting closer to perfect with each rewrite?" I asked.

She shook her head side to side, "I don't think so. That's what's frightening. Each time I rewrite, something seems to disappear."

"Are you saying the story is losing some of its freshness?" I asked.

"Yes, it feels sort of sanitized now. It's lost some of its punch. I don't know how to get it back." She put her elbows on the table and dropped her forehead in her hands.

Evelyn grabbed her friend's arm. "Find your original chapters and finish the story. That's all you need to do. Throw out those rewrites!" Evelyn was so anxious to help.

Thankfully, our meals arrived. I needed some time to think about the next right question. After a few minutes I forged ahead.

"Julia, do you have any idea why you're sabotaging your career?"

"Doing what?"

"Sabotaging your writing career."

"Sabotage! I'm not trying to do that! I just want it to be right before I put myself out there."

"You told me with each rewrite you've lost something. You didn't say it got better. If you're not moving forward, you must be going backwards, right?"

A flash of understanding crossed Evelyn's face and she spoke, "If you don't finish your book, you can't send it off. If you don't send it off, you'll never have to find out if it will sell."

Evelyn was right, of course, but I was hoping Julia could've discovered the truth for herself without any help from her friend. Too late.

"There are lots of reasons why people don't finish books," I said. "Some people are afraid the book will be rejected and they'll die of a broken heart. The flip side is risky too. If the book is published then they'll be expected to write another one. If a writer doesn't believe she'll ever get another idea as good as this one, then she'll hang on to the one idea for dear life. It's fear."

Julia took a big breath, exhaled and looked at me.

"Do you think you'll never have another idea as good as this one?" Evelyn asked Julia.

Evelyn was a quick study; she had just asked the next right question.

Julia nodded and looked intently at the remains of her pasta as she spoke. "I'm afraid this is the last good idea I'll ever have. I'm afraid this is my one and only chance to make it."

"Julia, is this novel the 'one and only' project you're working on right now?"

"Of course, I've given this book my full attention for over a year."

"Do you remember the Ed Sullivan Show?" I asked.

Julia looked at Evelyn and chuckled, "What does *that* have to do with anything?"

"Do you remember the plate spinner guy?" I asked.

"Sure, every Baby Boomer in America remembers him."

"Oh, yes!" Evelyn said. "That was a great vaudeville act and that crazy music the orchestra played in the background!"

"On the stage there was some sort of a platform that held several vertical poles, maybe eight or so. The guy waltzed on stage with a stack of white dinner plates. One at a time, with great flourish, he put a plate on top of a pole and started spinning it. He added one plate after another to the poles until there was a whole line of spinning plates. To keep all the plates spinning he had to watch them closely. He only tended the plates that were wobbly. If a plate dropped off, he put it back on and started it spinning it again. If a plate fell off and broke, no problem, he had a stack of replacement plates. Julia, can you see any reason why I would bring up the plate spinner?"

"I only have one plate?" she said.

I nodded.

"You've decided your novel is your 'one and only' plate. If you only have one idea it becomes too precious. If you had a whole line of 'plates' you wouldn't feel the need to obsess over this one. You could let it go because other plates need your attention too. It's too risky emotionally to only have one idea. If it breaks, all you'll have left is an empty stage. You don't have to live in that kind of fear. Your creative mind is capable of spinning new ideas all the time. You don't have only one perfect idea."

"You have lots of great ideas!" Evelyn said.

"Julia, do you believe you are a creative person?" I asked.

"Yes."

"Do you think that your creative mind is able to generate lots of ideas?

"Yes, I believe it can."

"Then wouldn't it stand to reason that you could trust the process to work for you one more time?"

"I guess it could."

"Now, tell me the idea you've been toying with for the sequel to this book."

Julia smiled. "Sequel? How did you know I was hoping to be invited to write a series?"

Julia told me about the next idea for her detective series, a murder set at an Oklahoma state park.

"Steal a little time away from your novel to outline your next mystery. It'll feel good to reassign some of your creativity to a new idea."

Julia smiled. "I think I can manage two plates spinning."

In writing it's important to not allow one idea to end without having another one waiting in the wings. If you find yourself obsessing over one idea you may be unable to let it go. Save yourself some anxiety and be a multiple plate spinner.

Before you finish a chapter, always begin the next one before you quit writing for the day. A few opening sentences will keep you from having to start from scratch the next time you sit down. That's just one way to prime the pump of your creativity and keep one step ahead of your creative self. Do yourself a favor and overlap projects—this will keep you in forward motion.

Here's a story told to me by my writing teacher, Peggy Fielding. There's a legend about a famous science fiction writer who wrote hundreds of short stories, books and magazine articles. This sci-fi writer wrote in the days before computers and word processors. He wrote on manual typewriters—typewriters, not typewriter. The walls of his office were lined with tables and desks. Sitting on each horizontal surface was one black typewriter. The exact number of typewriters is in question, so let's just say a dozen. Visualize twelve clunky manual typewriters lined up, ready for action like metal toy soldiers, ever ready for battle. The carriage of each typewriter held one sheet of paper. Each typewriter was devoted to a separate story or article.

This writer had a routine. He typed at least one line on each of those twelve typewriters before he called it a day. If he stalled out on one story and needed time to think over an idea, he simply rolled his squeaky metal office chair to another typewriter and worked his magic there. Day after day, year after year, he banged out his stories and articles. He always had at least twelve works-in-progress. This was the secret to his prolific career.

Before I decided to put this story in this chapter, I thought I needed to do some research. The librarian directed me to a book of memoirs written by this writer's second wife. Wife Number Two said she had heard the legend about the typewriters and it wasn't true. She said her husband had lots of typewriters, but they were not all out at the same time. She said he had a stack of extra typewriters in a closet just in case one quit on him, he would have a spare.

I told Peggy what I had discovered. Peggy said, "What would the second wife know? Find a book of memoirs by Wife Number One, she'll tell you the same story I told you." End of story.

We may never know for sure which story is true so you get to decide which version of the story works for you. I personally like the typewriters-lining-the-wall story—that version helps me remember to keep my creative juices flowing by working on several ideas at the same time. But the typewriters-stashed-in-the-closet version could work for you too. That story could remind you to keep a backup of your computer files or recharge your laptop battery so you can keep writing every day. Either way the point is the same: do whatever you need to do to keep writing—every day, no matter what.

And if you need another reminder that can be documented for accuracy, think back to that simple black and white world of the sixties when audiences applauded a man who kept a row of plates spinning.

Be Happy, Enhance Your Productivity and Creativity

A radio station played a short movie clip during the Monday morning rush hour. The drive time feature called "What's Your Favorite Part?" was a perfect example of how easy it can be to raise your spirits from ho-hum to happy. Maintaining an upbeat mood will enhance your ability to stay in your optimum creative zone. Cultivating and protecting good-feeling thoughts will create a temporary time frame of hopeful anticipation, excitement, happiness and joy. In this state of mind creative ideas flow naturally and when we're joyful, we're more productive.

The entertainment industry understands this feel-good concept and uses it to gain loyal fans and generate advertising dollars. For example, my radio station makes "happy" happen for listeners in the early morning darkness of Oklahoma winter. I admit, I'm not thinking thoughts of contentment at 7:00 a.m. on a Monday morning. My Monday morning thoughts run along this line: "The weekend went by too fast." "I hardly made a dent in my list of things to do." "I woke up late and now I have to rush to get to work on time." "Why is traffic so slow?"

The radio was on but I hadn't noticed the music; my inner thoughts were louder than the car radio. I wasn't in the mood to seize the day. As I pressed the accelerator in a futile attempt to make it through the intersection the D.J. announced, "It's time for 'What's Your Favorite Part?'" I turned up the volume. The station played an audio segment from the 1994 movie *Pulp Fiction*.

Two hit men, John Travolta and Samuel L. Jackson, are discussing McDonald's menu items. It had been years since I'd seen *Pulp Fiction* but I could still clearly visualize that scene.

"In Paris," John Travolta said, "You know what they call a Big Mac? Le Big Mac." I leaned forward, ready to hear the punch line. Jackson asked "What do they call a Whopper?" Travolta said "I don't know, I don't go to Burger King." I laughed out loud.

116

Experiencing a "favorite part" from a movie shifted my morning mood from tired and uninterested to happy and alert. The radio station gave me a free feel-good moment. My inner smile lasted well into the morning.

TV stations provide feel good moments too. Cable stations repeat popular movies from the 80's and 90's like *Mrs. Doubtfire, Forrest Gump, Pretty Woman,* and *Ferris Bueller's Day Off.*

Let's say I'm channel surfing and I click on a station showing *Mrs. Doubtfire.* Robin Williams dressed as an elderly nanny is standing in front of the stove cooking dinner. I know if I stay with the movie for a minute longer, his rubber bosom will catch fire and he'll put out the fire with pot lids. This scene makes me laugh every time so I willingly set aside whatever I was doing and sit down to watch this "favorite part." I laugh, I feel good and then I go on about my business. There's no reason to watch the rest of the movie, I've already seen it. I got what I needed—a feel-good moment.

I bet you've already envisioned your favorite part of that movie. What part do you like? The "drive-by fruiting?" When tipsy Mrs. Doubtfire loses her dentures in a glass of wine at a fancy restaurant? Your favorite part will make you laugh, no matter how many times you've seen it. It's a free feel-good moment.

Television execs choose to run movies with guaranteed consumer appeal. These movies haven't lost their charm; in fact, they're a part of our collective American culture. Most cable TV viewers have seen these popular movies many, many times over the years—or at least parts of them!

Ratings prove viewers tune in to watch their favorite parts for a quick feel-good moment. High ratings translate into increased advertising dollars. It's a win-win for everybody. We laugh in our living rooms. The TV execs laugh all the way to the bank.

But, as the radio station audio clip from *Pulp Fiction* illustrated, you don't even have to *see* your favorite part on the TV to experience a feel-good moment, you can simply hear it. In a conversation with friends any one of us could possibly even recite a favorite line from one of these popular movies and get the group

laughing. Here's one of my favorite lines: "Bueller, Bueller..."
Teachers love that one.

Remember, a good feeling can happen in many ways. You
don't have to see the movie again to get the good feeling. You
also don't have to hear the audio segment; you can talk about it
with a friend. You don't have to talk about it, you can just *think*
about it and replay the scene in your mind. Any of these
intentional efforts on your part can result in the same burst of
temporary happiness—the feel-good moment we all want!

In a feel-good moment, individuals can capture their fleeting
creativity and harness it. In this euphoric state of mind, however
temporary, we're more productive and that's when creative ideas
flow.

"Flow" is defined by Mihaly Csikszentmihalyi in his 1990
book by the same title, as a state of "optimal experience." Flow is
a time when ideas come easily and quickly. Solutions to problems
float into our consciousness, the next leap-frog jump of creativity
can be clearly seen. In this optimal experience time frame people
feel most creative. In flow, individuals often report being unaware
of the passage of large blocks of time due to their extreme
concentration and involvement in some enjoyable activity.

As an artist I've experienced the timelessness of flow in
workshops when my only responsibility was to make art. As a
writer I've experienced flow when I've explored a new idea. An
hour and a half at the keyboard felt like only a few minutes.
Although intense, experiencing flow is far from exhausting—it's
exhilarating. My son, the violist, will practice for hours at a time
and feel refreshed. The joy of doing what we love to do energizes
our inner spirits.

In the flow, we are at our creative best. We enjoy our
creativity. We're happy! We feel grateful for our creativity. We're
excited about the possibilities of the future and hopeful about all
we will create. We feel contentment. We feel happy, excited,
hopeful, content, and grateful.

I believe an individual is at his or her highest creative potential
when he or she feels happy, excited, hopeful, or content. These
emotions are set in motion when our inner self-talk and thoughts,

reflect gratitude, happiness, hopefulness, excitement, or a contented "everything will be fine" view of life.

Happy   Excited   Hopeful   Content

Thoughts create feelings. A happy feeling is a powerful reset button for your creativity. Think about it, it's hard to feel lethargic or uninterested when you're laughing or enjoying a friend's funny story. Happiness trumps all cards.

You've probably heard about Norman Cousins' book *Anatomy of an Illness.* Cousins believed human emotions were the key to fighting illness. Cousins fought his own heart disease and arthritis with massive doses of Vitamin C and Marx Brothers movies. He mixed up his own prescription cocktail of positive attitude, love, faith, hope and laughter. Cousins said ten minutes of genuine belly laughing gave him two hours of pain-free sleep. Laughter, happy thoughts and pleasant feelings created a physical and mental environment in which his health could improve, and it worked. Cousins lived years past his doctor's predictions.

Cousins took charge of his mental well being on purpose. He didn't wait until he felt happy to watch a funny movie. Watching a funny movie put him in a happy mood. Feeling better mentally helped him to feel better physically and as a result his health improved. Cousins took action to improve his life.

Feel-good moments can happen by accident like my drive time radio show or you can be proactive like Norman Cousins and create your own moment on purpose.

Here's my favorite way of hitting my reset button when I'm feeling discouraged about a writing project: *The Mask of Zorro.* I love Zorro. I have loved Zorro since I was a little girl. I am entranced by his black cape and mask. I adore his finesse and charm and his Spanish accent. Most endearing of all is Zorro's courage and bravado. He's able to right all wrongs in a swordfight and destroy injustice with the crack of his whip.

Watching the opening scene of *The Mask of Zorro* with Anthony Hopkins and Antonio Banderas will make me feel as if I could conquer the world. If Zorro's bravery can squelch the evil designs of villains and get a cheering crowd chanting his name, "Zor-ro, Zor-ro!" then I can certainly write another sentence.

I can watch the first few minutes of *Zorro* to feel excited and hopeful about life, but I don't need to watch the movie, I can simply sit still and replay it in my mind and the same effect occurs. I can hear the music from the soundtrack and that'll work too. I'm an absolute Pavlov's dog for Zorro!

I know Zorro's fiction. I know Zorro will never make love to me in his hidden underground lair of carnal delights, but those facts don't matter. The point is, I've found my reset button for discouragement and all I have to do is hit it and get on with my life. The next time I need Zorro's courage and bravado, I know where to find him. It's easy and it works for me every time.

You may have a favorite piece of music that will lift your spirits every time. Some people feel energized when they listen to the theme song from *Rocky*. I prefer Sebelius' *Finlandia*—that's two minutes and forty seconds of hope every time. Maybe you like rock music. I have a friend who said Queen's *Fat Bottomed Girls* gets him going when he's feeling low.

Figure out what works for you and use it. When you sense your mood is shifting into low gear, take charge and redirect it. Choose a Bible verse that encourages you. I can recommend Philippians 4:13 "I can do all things through Christ who strengthens me." Call a friend for a pep talk. Walk outside in the sunshine. Drink a glass of orange juice. Spend a few minutes with your pet. Identify your feel-good triggers and intentionally put them into action when you feel your mood drifting away from happy, excited, hopeful or content. This is a way to manage your mood so as to not disrupt your creative abilities.

Feeling good and feeling happy will temporarily shift your attention away from whatever ails you, whether that is illness or discouragement. Happy thoughts generate happy feelings—the perfect zone for being in the flow of your creativity. Creative people must take charge of their mental states to ensure more productivity and fun in their lives.

Happiness is an inside job and it's an inside job that pays big benefits. When you're feeling happy, your creative thinking skills are in tip-top form. You have energy to be productive. You can generate more ideas. You have a feeling of well-being that enables you to ignore the minor distractions of life and keep on working. Feelings come from thoughts. Happy feelings come from thinking happy thoughts. If you want to be in charge of your productivity and creativity, you must be willing to take charge of your thought life. Everybody knows negative self-talk will kill your confidence and hamper productivity. Make an intentional choice to manage your thoughts. Create your best mental environment.

In a workshop titled, "How to Ask the Next Right Question," I asked my participants to write all the emotions they could think of on the white board.

Here's the list: happy, fearful, excited, hopeful, anxious, nervous, overwhelmed, frustrated, disappointed, worried, content, bored, depressed, agitated, pessimistic, mad, sad, discouraged, hurt, angry, jealous, sorry, resentful, hopeless, guilty, grateful, insecure, impatient, gloomy, and sleepy.

I asked a volunteer to circle all the positive emotions in green marker and circle all the less than positive emotions in red marker. These emotions were circled in green: happy, excited, content, grateful and hopeful. The rest were circled in red.

"What does this list tell us about emotions in general?" I asked.

"There are more negative emotions than positive emotions," one special education paraprofessional said.

"How do you see negative emotions impacting your students?" I asked her.

"My students often feel overwhelmed, frustrated and discouraged about schoolwork," she said. "The worse they feel the harder it is for me to get them to participate in class. If they're having a good day, they do better."

"Let's look at the negative emotions," I said, "are they all equally debilitating?"

After some discussion the group concluded that boredom was not as serious as despair and didn't have the same long-term effects. Feeling insecure, while worrisome, could pass with some positive interactions with a teacher or fellow student.

"Once one of my students gets mad and angry," Catherine said, "It takes them a long time to cool off. For a while I have to really monitor their interactions with others until they settle down on the inside."

I asked the teachers to categorize the emotions into groups. Here were the results:

Group one: Excited, happy, hopeful, content and grateful are the most positive emotions. When individuals feel these emotions they're more able to handle the everyday nuisances of life, enjoy their peers, laugh and have a good time, and complete tasks.

Group two: Bored, pessimistic, frustrated and impatient are emotions shifting downward. They noted when a student feels bored it will take them longer to complete a task. Frustration and impatience about rules, restrictions or requirements often go together. Imagine a time when you were standing in a long line to make a return at Walmart. Each minute seemed like an hour. By the time you reached the front of the line you were cranky.

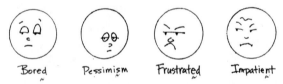

Bored   Pessimism   Frustrated   Impatient

Group three: Overwhelmed and tired were the emotions in the next grouping. When frustration covers over you and nothing you do seems to make things better, it's natural to begin to feel emotionally overloaded and very often, physically tired. Have you ever gone to bed and covered your head to escape the frustrations of the day?

Overwhelmed
Tired

Group four: When enough hardships block your path it's easy to feel that nothing will change. You may feel disappointed in life in a general and pervasive way. You could worry you're "in for a siege" (a favorite phrase of my mother's!). Discouragement follows.

Disappointed   Discouraged

Group five: When you feel hurt and sad you drift to a new low point. Friends seem to have deserted you in your time of need. There's a vague sense of loss. You begin to feel disconnected from life, a watcher on the outside.

Hurt
Sad

Group six: After hurt and sadness comes anger and jealousy. You feel defensive and push people away leaving you alone with your thoughts.

Angry.   Mad   Jealous

Group seven: In our perceived aloneness you begin to feel "less-than" and doubt your abilities. Anxious, insecure thoughts flood our minds. You dwell on mistakes from the past and feel guilty. Despair and depression shut you down.

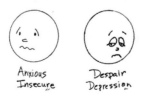

Anxious   Despair
Insecure   Depression

Think of these seven groups of emotions as the floors of a tall building. At the top floor the sky is blue, you can see for miles. You feel hopeful and happy. You think to yourself, "What a great day this is! I'm going to get so much done. I feel confident."

But if you take the elevator just one floor down, your mood shifts. All of a sudden you've noticed you're bored with your job. What your boss is asking you to do is beneath your abilities. The repetitive nature of some of the tasks of your work seems pointless.

Take the elevator down another floor and you're going to look for some time and for a place to take a snooze just to escape. You feel overwhelmed and tired.

One more floor down this emotional elevator and you begin to think "I should be farther along in my career than I am. I'm a disappointment to myself and my family."

One more floor down and you stop connecting with friends. You sequester yourself thinking you're not worthy. You're hurt and sad and nobody can talk you out of it.

At the bottom floor you doubt your abilities. Your thoughts run away with you. "Who do I think I am? I can't write a novel!" "Why would any gallery be interested in my paintings? They're trash!" "I can't sing. My grade school music teacher was right when she told me I couldn't tune a radio!" You feel anxious and insecure and the day looms ahead of you like a tornado cloud forming on an Oklahoma horizon.

In my work as creativity coach I often work with artists and writers fighting a temporary creative block. My goal is to have the person identify their feelings and the background thoughts that generated those feelings. Then I ask them the next right question over and over again until they can begin to feel hopeful about their future opportunities, excited about their creative work, happy with what they produce and content with the way their career is steadily progressing toward their stated goals.

Here's an example: A writer makes an appointment to talk to me.

"What do you want to talk about?"

"I'm depressed about my work," he said.

"What happened that made you feel depressed?"

"I got a rejection letter in the mail this past week."

"And you've been feeling down since then?"

"Yes, I haven't been able to do much." I can see he's depressed and inactive.

"What emotions do you feel when you think about that letter?"

"I think I must not be able to write at all. That rejection letter makes me want to quit." He's at rock bottom. He's lost his confidence.

"Before that letter arrived how did you feel about your writing?"

"I felt like I was doing good work. I was writing every day and feeling good about what I was producing, but all that changed when I got that damned letter!" He was definitely mad and angry.

"That kind of a letter can set you back temporarily," I said trying to interject the idea that his depression wouldn't go on indefinitely.

"Well, and I guess if I admit it, my feelings were hurt, *are* hurt. I was so sure I was going to get a break this time." He demonstrated hurt, sadness and disappointment.

"So what you're telling me is that this letter from someone you've never met has made you think you'll never get your work published?"

"Well, I don't know if I would go *that* far. The woman did actually sign the letter."

"That's excellent. That means it wasn't a total and complete rejection."

"Why do you say that?"

"The editor took the time to sign her name. My writing teacher in her last newsletter had some information about rejection letters. Peggy Fielding said 'There are gradations in rejections.'" He leaned forward to listen more carefully. "'A printed form,' Peggy said, 'is the lowest rung on the ladder. A printed form signed by a real person is a step above that. And a personal letter that mentions your book is the next step up.'"

"I think my letter was signed in blue ink!" He's excited.

"That's something to be proud of," I said, interjecting gratefulness.

"Wow! I got a signed letter from a publisher!" He's grateful and happy.

"How does that feel?"

"Good enough to send out another query. That letter wasn't so bad. I'm on the right track after all. These things just take time." The formerly depressed writer is hopeful and focused on his bright future.

With a few choice questions, our writer took the express elevator from the bottom floor to the penthouse. He moved up so fast he skipped two floors. He sailed past the third floor (overwhelmed and tired) and the second floor (bored and frustrated) and made his way straight to the top in record time. With a clear view of the vista from the top floor, he felt excited, happy, grateful and hopeful.

In my practice I direct my efforts to ask "the next right question." You can do the same for yourself. The first question to ask is "What am I feeling?" Identify the feeling and see where that feeling lands on the emotion list. If you're bored with your job for instance, it could be fairly easy to find something to be grateful for—friends you enjoy, access to a take-home laptop computer, health insurance, an office with a door. In no time, you're back on track. The first opportunity you have for a few minutes alone you might even find yourself typing on your novel!

Here are some action steps to get you going up on the creativity elevator.

- **Step 1**: Identify how you feel. Simply ask yourself, "How am I feeling?"
- **Step 2**: Check the list of emotions for a GPS location of your feelings. How far below happy, excited, content and hopeful are you right now?
- **Step 3**: Find out what happened. Ask yourself "What happened in my life that caused me to take this downward turn?" The answer to this question pinpoints a real event.
- **Step 4**: Ask "For what length of time do I choose to give my time and enthusiasm away to this event?" If you do

choose to stay in a blue mood for a while (you may want to have a mini or major pity party) then set a limit on how much time you'll give yourself to be mad, disappointed etc. Most likely asking this question will seem silly and you'll move on.

- **Step 5**: If you've decided to take charge of your thinking and subsequent emotions for the higher good of fun, productivity and creativity, then begin asking yourself clarifying questions that relate to each grouping of emotions. Work your way up question by question until you reach a more positive state of mind.

Asking yourself the next right question puts you in charge of your life. I learned how to recognize my own pessimistic thinking habits and patterns by reading Martin Seligman's book, *Learned Optimism: How to Change Your Mind and Your Life*. In this book he showed me how to retrain my thought processes to see the world through rosier glasses. In my coaching practice I incorporated Seligman's ideas to create my own technique of asking the "next right question."

I feel I should point out that people experiencing clinical depression or those with certain mental disorders may have more difficulty managing a downward spiral of emotions. Just thinking along more optimistic lines won't work in all cases. I am not a therapist or psychiatrist, only a coach and minister. My style of coaching people to better feelings is most effective with creative people in the middle of a temporary creative block.

Thoughts generate emotions. Emotions show up in our feelings. Taking charge of your thought life will change your life. Your thoughts come from inside *your* head. You are the thinker.

It's not so much what happens to us, but how we respond to what happens to us. Ask yourself the next right question to live your life to the fullest. Once you realize that you're the only one in charge of generating your thoughts and therefore you're in total charge of your state of mind, you'll have to take responsibility for yourself. Seeing the world in a more positive light can't hurt and it certainly might help.

After all, the only thing you have to lose when you feel down is valuable time to work on the things that give you joy. Make a decision to ride the elevator to the penthouse every day!

Gatekeeper Basics

Last Friday evening my husband was watching *The Bourne Supremacy* on TV. I was curled up on the couch deep into *Amazing Results of Positive Thinking* by Dr. Norman Vincent Peale. My younger son called my cell just before 10:00 p.m. Dash and I usually visit after his weekly lesson with his viola professor. I left the room to talk.

After a bit of checking in I asked him, "How was your lesson today?"

"It went well. My professor asked me to play the Brahms sonata for a master class on Monday," Dash said.

"That's wonderful!" A request to play for a guest professor was a coup in this mother's mind.

"Well, yes. I guess it is good, but I don't really want to do it," he said.

"It doesn't matter," I said.

"What do you mean it doesn't matter?" he asked.

"He's the viola guru. You're his lucky student. Whatever he tells you to do, you do."

"But, there's only one open time slot for the master class at 11:30. That's right after I have class and a music theory test. My accompanist has the same test. She's not going to want to play for a master class."

"Ask her anyway," I said. "It's important for you to play for this person, whoever he is."

"The master class person is a she; anyway, I Googled her name. I can't find much about her."

"It doesn't matter."

"What do you mean it doesn't matter?" he asked the same question again.

"It doesn't matter who she is or isn't. Just for the record, Google doesn't know everything. A search engine can't possibly know why your professor wants you to play for her. What matters is that your gatekeeper wants you to play for her."

"What's a gatekeeper?" Dash asked.

"A gatekeeper is anyone in a position of influence or power that can make things happen. Your professor is a gatekeeper to the world of professional music. He already lives there, you don't. Listen to him. Do what he says. Gatekeepers know people, they know about hidden opportunities and they love to offer them to people they think can make the most of the experience. Gatekeepers can steer you in the right direction. They can save you time. Gatekeepers can open doors for someone they believe has potential and drive. When a gatekeeper offers you an opportunity, take it. You don't have to understand why it's important, you just have to recognize if your gatekeeper thinks it's important, it's important."

"Mom, I'm not sure it's that big of a deal," It seemed Dash wasn't quite sure he wanted to make the effort on such short notice.

"How do you know when it's a big deal and when it's not?" I hate to admit I wasn't using my best coaching skills with my own kid. I didn't wait for him to answer my question. "Okay, what if your professor only asked you to play for this master class because this woman was a personal friend and he wanted her to hear one of his students. Wouldn't that be reason enough to prepare and play on Monday?"

"Well, yes, I guess it would," Dash said, "But he's also asked two grad students to play for her too."

"Nice company."

"Okay. You're right."

"Good. That master class could open a door to a new possibility. That half-hour could lead to something else on down the road. She might give you an important tip that will improve your technique. Two years from now she might hear of an orchestra looking for a violist and she'll give them your name. Maybe she's bringing her beautiful daughter with her and you're going to fall in love at first sight!"

He laughed. "Okay, okay, Mom."

I had just a little more to say. "Dash, if you choose not to play on Monday, nothing will happen. You close a door and you'll probably never know what you missed by not playing for her. You're on your own hero's journey."

I paused for effect. Dash was familiar with Joseph Campbell's *Hero's Journey.*

"The mentor offers the young hero a series of tests and quests. If you pass the test, you move on to the next test, finally there's the big prize. Everything counts in the hero's journey. Every new opportunity is a gift. The correct response when a gatekeeper gives you an opportunity is 'Yes, thank you so much for thinking of me!'"

"Mom! I'm convinced. I'll call my pianist. But what if she says she's too busy to get ready on such short notice?" he asked.

"Offer her twenty bucks. I'll put it in your account," I said.

"Thanks, Mom."

"Keep me posted. I've got a good feeling about this one."

"I know. Me too," he said.

At a workshop I was asked this question: "I'm a teacher and I want to write and publish. What should I do?"

My short answer was "Write and participate in an active writers' group. Basically, do what writers do and go where writers go."

Whether you want to write, paint, sing or drum, look for people with like interests. Breaking into any new area will require extra effort on your part; it's much like searching for a job—you need contacts, opportunity and drive.

To find connections, call the library. Most libraries keep a list of local clubs and organizations with contact phone numbers or website addresses. Call one of the officers and ask about their group and meeting times. Visit several clubs and see which one is a fit for your needs. If your time is limited and you can only attend one group, choose a group that meets year round with an emphasis on education and information. If your schedule allows, join an additional group for a social and networking outlet. Attend conferences and workshops. Go to lectures, gallery openings, book signings, and concerts. Talk to people in the business, ask questions, soak up all the information you can hold and do your creative work with everything you've got!

When feel sure you want to invest your time and energies in this creative field, keep your eyes and ears open to find the gatekeepers.

Gatekeepers are people in positions of power, but don't let titles confuse you; the real power person in a group may not be the President of the club or the chair of a committee. Very often the gatekeeper is a long-time member of the group with reams of experience, common sense and a small entourage of followers. The gatekeeper will be the go-to person. Gatekeepers make things happen. They know who to call to get something done quickly. A gatekeeper can pull strings because he or she has the strings.

The gatekeeper may be generous with his or her time or knowledge, if so, attend his or her workshops or classes. Attend his book signings or her gallery opening and lecture. Be regular in attendance at the club meetings where the gatekeeper is also a member. Say "Yes" to small volunteer jobs in the organization. Do your task with excellence, get it done on time and your efforts will be noticed. Say "Yes" to requests for your help as often as you can manage. Do the job cheerfully and to the best of your ability. If you need help, ask the gatekeeper for advice and take it to heart. Remember, you're the new kid on the block, the gatekeeper is the expert. Whenever and wherever possible, don't miss an opportunity to learn from the best.

You're on a hero's journey too.

P.S. I heard from my son later that same week. He left a voice message.

"Mom, I just wanted you to know I had my lesson today and it went well. My professor told me the lady I played for in the master class asked about me and commented on my tone. My *gatekeeper* was very proud."

I could hear the smile in his voice.

The Care and Feeding of Leapfrogs

I received this email question: "In past years I've worked as an artist and freelance writer. I've recently gone through a divorce and a move. Now that I'm feeling more settled I'm thinking about getting back to my creative work again, but I don't know what to do. The images I used to paint no longer excite me and old story ideas seem stale. Can you tell me how to find a new idea?"

My reply: You've asked the really big question: "How do I find inspiration?" Inspiration is not an 'X' on a treasure map. Inspiration is found along the way, as you are going; it's the journey, not the destination. Inspiration lies within. Your creative mind holds all the inspiration you'll ever need. Your creativity has not dried up or disappeared. It's still inside you, patiently waiting to be reactivated.

To uncover the ideas waiting to be birthed, ask yourself "What am I noticing?" Are you captivated by the color changes and cloud shapes in the sky? Your Muse may be calling you to paint a series of oversized landscapes full of weather and atmosphere. Have you found that you're more aware of conversations going on around you? Subconsciously you may be toying with the idea of writing a dialogue-heavy screenplay like *Sideways,* the 2004 movie starring Paul Giamatti. When you read a newspaper article about a murder or robbery do you wonder about the back story? True crime or mystery writing may be on the horizon for you.

Dr. Wayne W. Dyer in his book *Inspiration: Your Ultimate Calling,* (Hay House, 2006) said, "Become aware of anything that excites you... that is inspiration right in front of you, begging you to pay attention to that feeling. You have the ability to pursue it." Dr. Dyer recommends keeping a list of everything that captures your attention. Look at your list and ask yourself "What is calling me to action?" Choose to follow that lead and take action; begin writing or drawing or dancing and see where your action leads you. The creative process will naturally move or jump from one idea to the next.

Ideas will flow once you begin working again, but you may be reluctant to start. If it's been an extended period of time since you exercised your art and writing or other creative muscles you may be feeling a fair amount of anxiety about the current status of your creative abilities. Those of us who depend on a steady stream of new ideas for our livelihood and/or sense of purpose, will occasionally experience anxiety and fear—especially after a long absence from our creative work.

This type of performance anxiety arises in the moment just before you pick up a brush or pencil or place your fingers on the keyboard. Are you feeling a little rusty? Have you secretly wondered if you've lost your touch? Are you afraid to test the waters to find out if you can still generate that feeling of inner satisfaction from a job well done?

Your creativity will return when you set it in motion. Relief from the anxiety is just one action away. Einstein said, "Nothing happens until something moves." Make a move—draw one line, type one word.

Find a copy of Anne Lamott's book *Bird by Bird.* In the chapter titled "Short Assignments" she says, "...all I have to do is to write down as much as I can see through a one inch picture frame. This is all I have to bite off for the time being."

Take her suggestion and give yourself a short assignment. Write for twenty minutes. Give your creativity a boost by minimizing exterior distractions—turn off your phone, TV and radio. If you think absolute quiet is too deafening, select a quiet CD of instrumental music. Don't clog your auditory senses by interjecting lyrics into your brain. Do your best to totally focus on writing for twenty minutes.

You'll make more progress if you're unaware of the passage of time. Take off your watch and cover clock faces (put a sticky note over the digital clock in the corner of your computer screen). Set the alarm on your phone to ring in twenty minutes or use a digital timer. Sit at your computer and get comfortable.

Breathe deeply and release any unrealistic expectations of literary greatness for these twenty minutes. You don't have to write the cover piece for *Time*, try for just a sentence or two for starters—only as much as you can see through a one-inch picture frame. That's all you have to bite off for the time being. Take another full breath and begin. Write until your timer signals the end of the twenty minutes. At the end of that time take a five-minute break, then decide whether or not you'd like to write for another twenty minutes.

Get back into the swing of painting by treating yourself to the luxury of fresh paint, a new piece of paper or canvas and a full hour with no distractions. Begin by mentally recalling the sensual nature of art you experienced as a child. Do you remember the joy of a brand new coloring book? The slightly rough textured off-white pages and bold black lines gave me boundaries I could choose to keep or ignore.

Did you ever have a box of sixty-four Crayola Crayons with the "built-in sharpener"? Each time I sat down to color I lifted the yellow-orange lid of the crayon box and took a big whiff of the crayons! I'm smiling just thinking about the smell of those waxy sticks of color. I experienced the same kind of joy when I opened my pricey wooden box of ninety-six Caran d'Ache Swiss watercolor crayons. The rows and rows of bright colored sticks were so luscious I gasped with delight!

Take a few minutes to set up your palette and workspace before you begin work. Don't rush this set-up time. I'll share with you my watercolor ritual that eases me into a creative and anticipatory state of mind. Fill a container with sparkling fresh water. Swish your brush around and around in the water to make a little whirlpool. Watch the water swirl until the spinning finally stops and the surface of the liquid settles into a flat invisible sheet in the can. Close your eyes and place your hand flat on the surface of your paper and feel the texture—the rough coolness waiting for life to spring forth much like a field of prepared ground. Rush your waterlogged camel hair watercolor brush across your palette to steal a stream of liquid color. Touch your brush to the paper and relish the feeling of being a creator. You've just made a mark that has never existed before!

A word of caution: keep your artistic expectations in check. You don't have to paint the Sistine Chapel ceiling, thankfully that's already been done. All you have to do is soak a piece of paper with color. Play with the paint. Pull long strokes of color with a flat brush. Squiggle wavy lines of color with a big round watercolor brush. Paint a pool of water and drop colors into it just for the sheer magic of seeing the colors blend together. Remember the joy of painting?

Now that you're feeling creative, are you ready for some instructions on nurturing your creativity? I call this process "the care and feeding of leap frogs." I explain creativity to my students and coaching clients in this way—creativity jumps like a leapfrog. Incidentally, there is no such species of frog, although frogs are often called "leapers." I adopted this term from a children's jumping game my Camp Fire Girls troop used to play at camp. We called the game "leapfrog." In case you've never played leapfrog here's how it goes. Children line up in a row with plenty of space between each person in the line. Each child squats down on the ground making her body as small and compact as possible. The last one in line begins the game by leaping over the backs of each of the other children all the way down the row. Then he or she squats down and the child at the back of the line gets to play leapfrog.

Real frogs and toads leap, jump and hop at will and their movements are never 100% predictable. The frog may jump to the right or left, in one slow hop or ten fast hops. There are short jumpers and long jumpers. It may even stop, shut its eyes and patiently wait for you to lose interest and go on about your business.

Jumping is what frogs do. Generating ideas in leapfrog fashion is what your creative brain likes to do. This is what the artistic process is all about—process not product. Allow your creativity the freedom to jump from one idea to the next. If given plenty of space and time, frogs will jump. Don't try to rush a frog along by poking or prodding. Frogs only jump when they are ready in the same way creative ideas will float to the surface of your conscious mind when you're ready to receive them. Don't restrict your frog by putting him in a box. Be willing to let your frog do what frogs do best and you'll be pleasantly surprised at where he may lead you.

Your leapfrog may be a right jumper or a left jumper. To use a political analogy, a left jump by your leapfrog may indicate your creative mind's interest in a new personally untested "liberal" blue route. If you've been toying with the idea of trying something totally new, your frog may be taking a turn to the left.

A right-jumping frog could mean you need to spend some more time with ideas already in process. Perhaps you've hit some sort of a creative snag with an idea and you've been thinking about abandoning it out of frustration or boredom. Your frog's persistence in maintaining his ground firmly in that well-traveled "conservative" red zone may mean he's insisting you stay the course and work through your current creative problem. A right jumping frog means there's more to do before moving on. Don't dismiss your current idea as being no longer valid. Push the envelope a little more to see what breaks through.

Here's a personal example of one of my leapfrog experiences. Each year I attend the Oklahoma Fall Arts Institute at Quartz Mountain State Park near Lone Wolf, Oklahoma (yes, Lone Wolf is as remote as the name suggests). The Fall Arts Institute is a major perk for Oklahoma public school teachers. Participants can choose between a wide variety of classes in the arts such as ballroom dancing, acting, sculpting, painting, creative writing, poetry etc. For four wonderful days each year I experience all the creative freedom of my college years: unrestricted time and studio space to explore new ideas. It's heaven! No responsibilities except to let my leapfrog jump!

This past fall I was a student in a mono-printing class taught by Marwin Begaye, printmaking professor at The University of Oklahoma in Norman, Oklahoma. In the first class session Marwin taught the basics of the mono-printing process and gave instructions on how to use the printing press; then he stepped to the side and made himself available for questions or suggestions. Marwin trusted the process and us. He knew we could all find our own way.

In those free hours of playing with a new medium I found myself printing layers of deep rich colors with simple shapes etched into the thick ink. To my surprise I was creating abstract art, a first in my long career of being a representational painter fond of figure studies. My frog had taken a sharp left turn and I enjoyed the new scenery.

This past year my husband and I went to New York City to see my son play in a concert at Carnegie Hall. What a magnificent experience for a parent! While we were in the city we visited several museums including the Metropolitan Museum of Art and the Museum of Modern Art. At the MOMA I was drawn to the Mark Rothko abstracts. The size of his paintings and the depth of color mesmerized me. In a flash I understood the connection between the images I'd printed in October at Quartz

Mountain and the extra large canvases of this abstract master. In an entire museum filled with famous artwork, my leapfrog led me straight to Rothko. I'm keeping a close eye on my frog, I'm anxious to see where he takes me next!

I also have a long relationship with my right jumping leapfrog. She keeps me busy reinventing the same image I've been painting for years—portraits of Mary, the mother of Jesus. In 1999 my leapfrog led me to the chapel at St. Johns Hospital in Tulsa, Oklahoma, where I stood face to face with an especially compelling Italian statue of the Blessed Virgin.

Since my introduction to Mary, portraits of her are a staple in my artistic repertoire. My first representations of Mary were realistic drawings based on photographs I'd taken of Mary statues from Catholic churches and Catholic hospitals in Oklahoma. Over the years my images of Mary continue to evolve. I change media and experiment with paper size. I no longer recreate photographic images of Mary; now I know her so well I draw her from my imagination. My drawings and paintings of Mary are visual prayers, my *thank you* to God for gifting me with artistic talent.

I have several leapfrogs active in my creative life, two artsy frogs (one blue and one red) and two literary frogs. One writer frog is happily following a non-fiction path and the other is

sneaking off into the realm of inspirational fiction. Keeping up with my leapfrogs means I'm never bored.

Simply put, your choice as a creative person is to follow the leading of your frog or not. Ideas will jump if given plenty of room, no time pressure and an open mind. Negative thinking, unrealistic expectations and anxiety will surely limit your frog's hopping abilities. Let your frog exercise regularly and stretch his or her legs. I once told a client who was quick to discount every creative idea as inconsequential, "Don't break your frog's legs!"

Is there a shortcut in the creative process? If there is I haven't found one. As an artist and writer I wish I had the secret to predicting the next tipping point idea. For a sociological view of why some ideas fly and others fail, I recommend two books by Malcolm Gladwell: *The Tipping Point: How Little Things Can Make a Big Difference* and *Blink: The Power of Thinking Without Thinking.*

Following your own creative path is the only sure way I know to find your next best idea, but whether that next best idea is marketable or not is a whole other conundrum.

I can offer one piece of advice for artists: one of the surest ways to kill creativity is to ask "Will this sell?" This is a loaded question because it invites premature editing of your creative ideas. If your only concern is to sell a piece, you may discount the value of the time spent in artistic exploration. You may decide in your mind that your current idea is not "good enough" to try. How can you be sure?

Before you discount an idea give it a little attention and effort. Play with it, give it some time, and see if it leads you to another idea. The creative process takes what it takes. Creative work is oftentimes a struggle, but worth it. The only way to arrive at your next great idea may be *through* the route of another idea.

Did you know American Abstract Expressionist Jackson Pollock painted lines for years before he perfected his signature "drip" line paintings in the late 1940's? Recently I saw museum gallery collection of Pollock paintings. Lines were the common element in all his works. The paintings were arranged chronologically. A quick left to right glance around the gallery made it easy to see how his line paintings changed and evolved over time to become his large signature "drip" paintings.

On closer inspection I saw evidence of Pollock's creative struggle. There were subtle changes from one canvas to the next. Over time the size of his paintings increased. With each jump in size, his primary images decreased in size as he made the decision to zoom in on the beauty of the line, recognizable images eventually abandoned.

Pollock applied his paint in a very active manner dubbed "action painting." Dancing around the edges of his canvases spread on the floor of his studio, Pollock worked his painting from all angles. His favorite paint was enamel house paint, more liquid and less expensive than artist's traditional oil paint. Enamel could be splashed and thrown. Contrary to popular thought, Pollock's lines were not totally random. He adjusted the dripped or thrown paint lines to get the exact width and texture of line desired. Pollock was determined to find the "look" he had in mind.

When I try to explain the creative process to my students I recommend they watch Ed Harris as Jackson Pollock in the movie *Pollock* (2000). In my favorite scene from the movie Pollock is painting in his studio. His large canvas was spread across the floor. With a can of enamel paint in his hand and a cigarette dangling from his lips, he paints lines of enamel paint onto his canvas with a large oil painting brush. As he is holding his brush in mid-air thinking about his next stroke, paint drips from his paintbrush onto the canvas creating a line. You can almost see the light bulb go off over his head!

Every creative action has value. Every idea will leapfrog to another. The creative process is an adventure. It can meander from a seemingly unpromising idea to a blockbuster creation in a flash.

Don't let your bank account balance influence you to abandon or discount an idea too quickly. Don't let your need to make a sale push you to play it safe and copy an image you've already sold. You may be surprised. It might not sell. An overused or overworked image can lose its "something special" quality. If your goal is to create a saleable image quickly and get it out the door, you may be selling yourself short. You might even feel personally less satisfied with your artistic efforts even if the image sells. Don't opt out of the full adventure and struggle of creation.

On the flip side, marketability is important. Creative people work and must make a living. Artists and writers paint and write because they're artists and writers and because they need to pay the mortgage, put food on the table, finance orthodontia for their children and pay years of college tuition. Artists and writers also work for paint, printer cartridges, and workshop registration fees and because it's enjoyable to do what you love.

How do you balance supporting a family and supporting your creative needs? We all hope to find a creative product or service that's both marketable and profitable. You're very fortunate when you find a frog that feeds you instead of you having to feed him! Your "cash" frog may be painting portraits or writing a syndicated newspaper column. Even if your work is repetitive and predictable you have a personal and professional responsibility to do your job to the best of your creative ability each and every time. Your client or employer will expect your finished product to be fresh and creative, full of life. The challenge for any creative person is to find ways to make your life's work creatively fulfilling when the novelty is gone. This can be done by having additional frogs *on the side*.

When I was a student at William Woods College in Fulton, Missouri in the 1970's I had an elderly art history professor who taught art history at 8:00 a.m. in the pitch-black basement of the art building. It was a tough time slot for sleepy students to try to stay awake for slides of Corinthian columns and Renaissance masterpieces.

Mr. Latta was a small man with a soft voice who clearly loved teaching art history but was not an engaging teacher. He spent a lot of his time in his office drawing pastel portraits of pretty young college girls. I was thrilled when he asked me to sit for him. He told me to come dressed in my favorite outfit. For my portrait I chose to wear a black formal from high school. It was an elegant dress with yards and yards of black net fabric.

For several Saturday mornings I came to his tiny office in the art building. The only light in the room came from a dusty glass window with the coveted north light. He rarely spoke. The only sound was the scratch of chalk drawn across the surface of the paper. His pursed lips were set in a horizontal line of concentration. Standing at his easel he stared at me with squinty eyes, taking mental notes on skin color and expression, and then he would shift his gaze to his easel and work. Occasionally he rested and smoked a big cigar. All morning long he drank massive amounts of black coffee in a dingy white porcelain cup that didn't look like it had ever been scrubbed clean—only occasionally rinsed out. The pleasure he seemed to derive from his lukewarm coffee suggested to me that it was fortified with something more interesting than sugar.

On the day Mr. Latta completed my pastel portrait he drew the letters of my first name in the lush red-violet background. It was a lovely portrait and my mother was happy to purchase it. It hung in the formal living room of my parent's home for many years until I finally talked her into letting me have it.

My professor had two "cash" frogs: teaching art history and painting pastel portraits of students. Each portrait was similar in style but uniquely different. He also had a third frog—a leapfrog interested in making small sculptures out of cut metal. I own two of Mr. Latta's figure studies in sheet metal. I'm pretty sure he sold more portraits than sculptures, but I also would wager he enjoyed being a metal sculptor just as much if not more than being a portrait artist. My art history professor lived a creative "both/and" life as an artist. The lesson? Keep several frogs—one or two that feed you and your family and another one that feeds your creative spirit.

In contrast, asking "Will this sell?" may be precisely the right question for writers. Testing the potential of your idea by sending a query letter before putting in too much time at the computer is the best avenue to success. Why waste your time and energy if your idea doesn't have an interested buyer? My writing teacher, Peggy Fielding, and my publisher, Dan Case, both advocate writing for *dollars*—not for self-actualization!

On the flip side of this argument, many writers manage to do both—writing when an editor or publisher has given the okay to continue and writing with no known buyers in sight. You may do both too.

Salvatore Lombino, wrote under the name Evan Hunter and Ed McBain. Ed McBain wrote the "87th Precinct" detective novels and Evan Hunter wrote the screenplay for Hitchcock's *The Birds*. My favorite British mystery writer, Ruth Rendell, reinvented herself as Barbara Vine. Do you have some steamy, fantasy, supernatural romance up your sleeve that you're afraid to write until your grandmother dies? Release your fears and your alter-ego frog. Adopt a pen name! Live a richer "both/and" life by using all the parts of your creativity.

Your leapfrog's main business is jumping and your main job is to follow his lead. Leapfrogs always want to take you places you've never been before. Take care of him; that leapfrog is your ticket to adventure!

PART IV:
Good Skills for Living

Center Yourself

David writes a weekly sports column for their town's newspaper. His wife, Patsy, takes commissions for pet portraits in pastels. As working parents of two small children, sons ages three and five, David and Patsy's evenings were consumed with cooking, child care and chores.

David emailed me searching for a way to build in time in their evenings to allow them time to work on their creative projects. I suggested a job-share arrangement. While Patsy cooked dinner, David played with the boys. After dinner, Patsy worked in her studio while David cleaned the kitchen and bathed the children. In an hour, Patsy took over bedtime duties and chores and David went to his office to write. By nine p.m. the kids were asleep and the adults had some time to catch up with each other or watch some TV.

As far as I knew, things were working out fine until I received his latest email question.

"I've successfully rearranged my evenings to allow about an hour to work on my writing, but when I sit at my computer I feel nervous and hyper. My brain races with negative self-talk. I can't seem to get started. What would you suggest?"

David's latest email told me he had time to work, but anxiety and negative thinking were limiting his productivity. In order to begin writing, David had to clear his mind before he could focus on the task at hand. With a weekly deadline, he knew he couldn't waste any time getting started. He felt pressured. In order to write with clarity and speed, David needed to feel calm and confident.

David thought he was having trouble *starting*, but I wondered if his real problem was *stopping*.

I replied: Have you ever seen a potter working on a potter's wheel? The clay has to be "centered" on the wheel before the potter can create a bowl or vase. In the same way your mind must be centered before you can begin your creative work. In order for you to make the most of your time, you must be mentally centered, physically calm and confident.

Here's a breathing exercise that will help you *stop* rambling thoughts and nervous body energy so you can *start* positive action on your writing.

I've modified a breathing exercise created by Eric, Maisel, author of *Coaching the Artist Within.* You'll need a note card, a non-digital clock with a second hand and three minutes of your time.

- **Step one**: Sit at your work place. Take a moment to listen to your self-talk. Replace any negative thought with a short phrase to positively address your fear or feeling. Some suggestions: 'I am calm and centered,' or 'Now is the time to begin.'

  Note the phrases are written in the present tense—*I am* calm and centered. *Now* is the time to begin. Write your short sentence on a note card and place it in view at your workplace.

- **Step two:** Look at the clock. Watch the second hand tick by for one minute. This will focus your attention on every second of the minute. When the second hand reaches the "12" take a deep breathe and hold for five full seconds until the second hand reaches "1" then exhale forcefully through your mouth for five seconds. Repeat until you have completed sixty seconds.

- **Step three:** During the next minute breathe normally as you watch the second hand circle the clock face. Mentally repeat your phrase. You may find your phrase will naturally break into two parts to match your inhale and exhale.

- **Step four:** In the next minute breathe in for five seconds and out for five seconds. You'll be surprised how much concentration it takes to keep your breathing timed and controlled (and you may find your brain is too engaged to generate negative self-talk!). In just a few minutes you'll feel centered, relaxed and ready to work.

Take control of your work time by coming to a complete *stop* before you *start* and your remaining time will be more productive. Centering your mind can be achieved by a breathing routine. In a very few minutes oxygen floods the brain and energizes your thinking. Take time to care for yourself. It's time well spent.

You probably can think of other positive ways to calm and center yourself. Here's a list of fifteen low or no-cost stress reducing/calming activities that will help you stop and slow down, so you can start a new activity.

When you feel anxious and nervous and need to get on task:

Sit in a comfortable chair and drink a cup of hot tea.

The aroma of the tea and the steam coming up toward your face are both calming. The hot cup warms your hands and feels comforting.

Comb a pet.

I have cats and dogs. Any of my pets would be grateful to have my undivided attention for some grooming. I get the added benefit of seeing their love expressed to me.

Walk around the block.

A brisk walk floods the brain with oxygen. Exercising your arms and legs will reduce tension in your neck and shoulders.

Read the comics.

This is an intentional way to release some laughter. Steer clear of the editorial cartoons though. The point is to relax, not get agitated!

Take a hot shower or relaxing bath.

The steam and soothing water release your bodily tensions. I find solutions to perplexing problems often come to me while I'm in the shower. That's why I keep a pad of paper and a pencil just outside the shower door to record my thoughts and ideas.

Listen to a recording of a favorite piece of music.

Find a piece that calms or inspires you. Imagine you're in a concert hall hearing a full orchestra playing that piece just for you.

Read a Psalm from the Bible.

I can recommend Psalms 8, 46, 63 and 90. For a special treat read these aloud in the elegant King James Version. You'll feel as if you've gone back in time.

Read a poem.

Any selection from Gibran's *The Prophet* or perhaps your taste runs to another kind of poet. Test poetry's limits. Poetry cannot be read quickly, enjoy the slow pace and absorb all the beauty in the words.

Rub lotion into your hands.

Do this in a slow meditative fashion. Imagine you're getting a manicure. Choose a lotion with a pleasant scent.

Eat an apple or orange.

Cut the apple into pieces. Arrange the pieces on a plate like spokes on a wheel. Place the orange segments in this same radial balance design. The visual beauty of this arrangement will encourage you to eat the pieces mindfully without rushing.

Run your fingers or toes through a dishpan of uncooked white rice.

This exercise was recommended by my physical therapist. Buy three pounds of uncooked white rice. Dump the rice in a dishpan until the depth of the rice is about three inches. Slowly pick up handfuls of rice and watch the rice fall through your fingers. Sweep your fingers across the surface of the rice. Stretch your fingers and grip handfuls of rice. Do this exercise with bare feet and you have a mid-western alternative to a walk on the beach!

Color a page in a coloring book.

I've discovered lots of adults will color if given a chance. Splurge and buy yourself a box of sixty-four Crayola Crayons and a coloring book. Choose a coloring book from the book section of your local discount store or toy store. If you're artsy, some museum shops carry coloring books with line drawings of famous paintings. Dover publishes an art coloring book, *Art Masterpieces to Color, 60 Great Paintings.* Coloring is relaxing, so is doodling and drawing. Let your imagination play with color and line.

Play a game of Checkers with your child.

A game of Checkers will usually only take a few minutes. The time you spend with your child will enrich your relationship and build his or her thinking skills.

Look at a photo album from a favorite vacation.

Remembering good times will create good feelings in the present.

Rock in a rocking chair or swing in a porch swing.

The steady rhythmic action works for colicky babies and may also work for you.

To center yourself you must allow yourself a chance to slow down, not rev up. Think of it in the same way you allow your system to slow down in order to fall asleep. Design your own list of ways to self-soothe and center yourself.

The key to centering yourself is to create a time gap between what you were doing and what you want to do. The brain needs a resting spot before it can successfully and smoothly change gears.

Optimistic Visualization:
Focus On What You Want

"Your vision will become clear only when you look into your heart. Who looks outside, dreams. Who looks inside, awakens."
Carl Jung

Cathy was an artist squarely in the middle of a major creative block. She was stuck. Cathy was a free e-coaching client assigned to me during my creativity coaching training. She lived in another state. The agreement was to correspond exclusively through email—no phone calls, and no face-to-face interaction for sixteen weeks. During this time the coaching client could stop coaching at any time.

My ministerial training and my experience in pastoral care taught me how to listen with my ears and my eyes. I use these same skills in creativity coaching. I listen to words spoken, tone of voice, body language and the silence. I call this time of silence "the gap." The "gap" is the pause between the "now" and the "not yet." The "now" is the "aha!" moment that arises from the right question at the right time or from a new inner understanding. The "not yet" is the moment directly following the "aha" moment when the person reflects on what has been revealed and considers what to do next.

In coaching or counseling the client brings a concern or has a question to begin the conversation. "Conversation" suggests a quick paced exchange between the coach and client. In face-to-face coaching, questions are asked, possible solutions are discussed and plans made.

In email coaching, without tone of voice, body language or silences, response time is slowed. Once I pose a question the client can hit "reply" and respond promptly or not. He or she can take days or even weeks to answer or simply choose to withdraw from coaching. The client can stop the conversation at any time.

Cathy taught painting workshops at conventions and regional meetings in the Northeast. She had several deadlines looming. She was participating in some sort of a competition as well. The image she entered had to depict spring. This elusive image of "spring" was the cause of her creative block.

At the end of her first email she said, "I don't feel creative. I want to be. I want to find inspiration. I want to move ahead and be more than I am. I hope you can help me. I really don't know where to start."

I really didn't know where to start either. I had lots of questions for Cathy but no easy way to get the answers. I tried to read between the lines of her emails. Cathy said she wanted to feel creative. She worked night and day on designs for competitions but she said she didn't "feel" creative. As an artist I've done commissioned watercolors that pleased my client but didn't please me as the artist. If Cathy only painted when she needed an example for one of her workshops then I could understand why she was having trouble digging deeper to find an original design.

Cathy was creative, but she lacked confidence in the creative process. She was so stressed she couldn't trust the process enough to believe that the right idea would surface "in time." Cathy was like a kid who pulls on a plant to try to make it grow faster. Her anxiety was undermining her efforts.

I also found it curious that she would write that she wanted to be "more than I am." A "more than" statement indicates a "less than" belief. Maybe Cathy was afraid her spring theme design wouldn't measure up to the expectations of her peers?

There was so much I didn't know about Cathy. I wished I could have had an hour to talk with her in person. I was afraid her fear of never finding the perfect design by her deadline would destroy her confidence.

Cathy was confused about what was important in her life and what was urgent—there's a difference. Cathy knew it was important to grow as an artist and she wanted to find ways to boost her own creativity, but she had chosen to let the urgent hold power over her. She thought this one piece of art would make or break her reputation in her organization. If she created the perfect design and earned her certification then she clinched her position as workshop leader extraordinaire. If she couldn't find the right design then she was sure she was down the tubes. "If/then" thinking is never based in reality. My problem was to try to help her relax so her creativity could blossom again. Attending to the important could solve her urgent problem.

In the beginning weeks Cathy emailed often. She told me she searched every day for an idea. She spent hours in the children's section of the library looking at books. She went to antique malls to look through stacks of vintage postcards. Cathy lived with high anxiety. Here's how I imagined she felt every day: you have an important job interview and your car keys are nowhere to be found. You look in all the usual places first, and when you can't find the keys what do you do? You turn right around and look in all the same places again, hoping you'd overlooked them. Only when you stop and calm yourself are you able to ask, "Where else could I look?" Cathy needed to look somewhere else. To find the spring design idea she had to look inside, not outside.

Cathy's anxiety reminded me of my own problem of misplacing things. I misplace my keys, credit cards and important papers. I keep papers in stacks and piles—not drawers and files! I don't like to say I've "lost" something because that sounds so permanent. I prefer to believe I have a temporary problem that will soon solve itself. I frame my search for the elusive item in this way: I say to myself, "It's not lost; I just don't know where it is right now." This is a little game I play to keep my anxiety low. When my husband sees me shuffling through stacks he calmly says "It's always in the last place you look." He's right.

The last place Cathy needed to look was inside. I emailed Cathy a question.

"Cathy, how do you feel each morning?"

She wrote, "I feel like I'll try and try again today and still won't find a design."

I replied, "Have you ever heard the phrase, 'Focus on what you want, not what you don't want'? Would you be open to a visualization exercise to help you change the way you view the day ahead?"

She said she was open to the idea.

I sent Cathy a version of the following visualization exercise which has been modified to apply to both artists and writers.

Optimistic Visualization

Clearly visualizing the desire of your heart will create an opening for the vision to manifest. Once you state a goal for your day you begin to become intentional about your actions, attitudes, thoughts and choices. Begin by being thankful. Be grateful for your creativity, talents, skills, education, and opportunities for success. Be thankful for your friends, family, health and home. Say a silent "thank you" for the gift of this day. Gratefulness opens your heart to receive more and accept more.

Your mind is brimming with creativity waiting to be released. Clear a path for your creativity. Guard your heart and mind from interior and exterior distractions. This day is too precious to waste a moment of it on negative self-talk or discouraging naysayers. This is the perfect day to create. Every minute of every day is a gift from God, given to you to with love so that you can grow and learn and become the person you were created to be.

Your future begins within your mind right now. Focus on what you want. See the future you want to live. What will you accomplish today? Imagine the joy and relief you will feel when you experience "flow." Focus on what you want. Focus on visualizing a future that is only moments away. You're already feeling a surge of ease and confidence bubbling up. You feel completely prepared to give birth to your creative ideas. Everything you need is already within you. Focus on what you want.

Begin the visualization exercise seated in a comfortable chair.

Feel the weight of your body supported by the chair.

Close your eyes and take a few deep breaths. Concentrate on lowering your shoulders with each exhale.

Place the palm of your hand over your heart. Be still. Feel your heartbeat.

Place your hands on your legs with fingertips close to your knees. Concentrate. Can you feel your heartbeat in your fingertips resting against your legs?

In your mind's eye stand and walk to your workspace.

Before entering the room, touch the light switch.

Do you believe that you must understand the nuances of electricity before the power will come on?

Do you believe when you flip the switch on the room will be illuminated in light? Try it and see. Did the light come on?

Now place the palm of your hand over your heart. Be still. Feel your heart beat. Do you believe creativity is like electricity?

Your creativity can be on or off. The power is available at all times. All you have to do is flip the switch on.

Decide to turn your creativity on. Flip your creativity switch on.

Move to your worktable, easel or computer.

Sit down. Pick up your pencil or paintbrush or put your fingers on the keyboard.

State your intention for this time set aside to work. Use the present tense.

"I'm painting a spring scene. My ideas are rich with possibility," or "I'm writing a paragraph. My character's personality will be revealed by the choices he makes in the midst of conflict."

Take a breath. Inhale and exhale slowly while you repeat a phrase that will allow your self-confidence to emerge such as: "I have all the skills I need to do my work today. I'm ready to begin," or "I understand the techniques and processes of my craft. I can do this."

Look at the white paper or canvas or the white screen of your document. Move your hands with confidence. Type a word. Make a mark with your pencil. Paint a brushstroke. Begin your work with confident action.

Do you see how one line flows into another? An image is beginning to emerge on your paper. What are your lines becoming? What story are you telling?

Be thankful for what is appearing before your eyes. It's a great beginning!

Open your eyes and go to your workspace. You're ready to start.

A few days later I received an email from Cathy. On July 29th she wrote, "Even though I'm doing your exercise I can't see my image yet. I know that I have to keep trying and that something will come."

Well, I'd given it my best shot. I had to trust the process too.

I didn't hear from her again until the first day of September.

"Just wanted you to know I have been successful with each of the designs I sent in to the committee. I'll be teaching one of my new designs at the next convention. Have a great weekend. Cathy."

That was the last time I heard from Cathy. She solved her urgent problem and finally found her spring design. Her email note sounded positive and I'm hopeful she found a way to look inside for her answers.

Time and Space Management

Susan was a successful commercial artist in a mid-sized town. I'd been invited to do a workshop. Susan made an appointment for an hour of coaching. We met in a café. The hostess seated us in a corner booth.

"Coffee?"

We both nodded yes.

"What would you like to talk about?" I asked.

Susan identified her problem areas to be time management and shrinking profits.

"Are these long-standing problems for you or something new?"

Our waitress appeared with two cups of coffee and cream. Susan smiled at her. The waitress greeted her by name.

"When I see clients I meet them at this coffee shop." Susan explained. "To answer your question, I've always had a problem with managing my time, but drifting into the financial red is new. Late last year I moved my business into my home."

"How's the switch to a home office working for you?"

She looked down and stirred her coffee for a moment before she answered. "Expenses are lower, but I'm not seeing more income. There are a few downsides to working out of my house that I didn't anticipate."

"What sort of downsides?"

"Here's a perfect example." She waved her hand around the restaurant. "I meet clients here because my home is too much of a mess. I've got art supplies all over the place and too many books. I still haven't had time to set up a filing system. There are stacks of boxes to unpack from the move. Who knows when I'll get to that, I'm always so far behind." She sighed and took a sip of her coffee.

"Anyway, I meet clients here and I pick up the tab. A couple of coffees and tip adds up over the month. It's a small expense, I know, but it's an expense I didn't have at the office on Main."

"Do you think buying coffee for clients is the problem?"

"No, the coffee isn't a big deal. It's part of the problem though. The real problem is time. When I had an office I didn't have to go anywhere to see clients, they came to me. If they were late it was no big deal. Now I have to stop what I'm doing and allow time to drive here. Sometimes I have to wait for clients to show up. That's dead time. Meetings take longer over coffee too. After the meeting I often stop on my way home to run an errand. Before I know it, I've lost an hour and derailed my train of thought. When I had an office I worked until the client showed up. We had a short meeting and when it was over I walked down the hall to my office and got right back to work. There was no down time. I had lots of billable hours."

Susan ran her fingers through her hair, sighed again, and looked out the window.

"Tell me more about how working out of your home complicated your life."

"A home office sounds great *if* you're the kind of person who can keep everything separated. Having my office in my home, means my home is my office. What I guess I'm really saying is that my business has taken over my home and my life. I'm not making enough money either. Everything is all mixed up. I know it's my attention deficit problem, but here's an example of a typical half hour: I do some work; I fold some laundry or notice dog hair on the carpet and think it's the perfect time to run the vacuum. It's crazy! All my mail, business and personal, comes to the house. Email is biggest problem. Clients send me email in the evenings and I'm dumb enough to answer! My house is a mess, my life is a mess, and so is my business."

Susan looked exhausted. Our waitress came to our table and lifted the coffee pot as if to ask a question. We both accepted a small warm up.

"I wouldn't have been able to anticipate all those problems with a home office. Sounds like it was a great idea in theory, but not so great in practice?"

"Yeah. When I had a real office, I worked while I was at work. It was easy to bill my time. I didn't take work home either. I had a life. I went out to dinner with friends. I even did some artwork for fun. Not now! I'm too far behind on my jobs to go out in the evenings or the weekends."

Susan noticed she was speaking too loudly for a restaurant. She leaned closer and whispered, "My income is down because I can't figure out how to bill people for my time, so I charge less than I probably should. I suspect that's how I'm going under one job at a time."

"Are you committed to keeping a home office?"

"For the time being I'm stuck. My income is down too much to pay rent."

"Okay, do you want to brainstorm some ways you could restructure your business practices?"

"That's why I'm here." I pulled out a legal pad for notes. In just a few minutes with a nudge or two from me, Susan started solving her own problems. I recorded her ideas. Susan wanted to tackle the mess in her house first.

"At the beginning, I had my home office so neat and organized. It looked like *Mission Organization* on HGTV."

"I'm familiar with that show. Think you can put it all back together again?" She tipped her head to the side and made a grimace. "Why not ask an organized friend to work with you for a few hours on a Saturday? The goal for that day is to put your business back in the office and shut the door."

"It'll be so nice to have my home back."

"Exactly, you need to be able to relax at home and work at your office—even if your office is in your home, this is possible."

"I think so too. Now, help me figure out a way not to have to work all the time."

"Tell me the hours you used to work when you had an office in town."

"I worked nine to six with a half-hour or hour for lunch if I met with a client."

"Make a sign for your office door that states your hours: nine a.m. to six p.m. Monday through Friday."

"And put it on the door inside my house? That's silly. I'm the only one who would see it!"

"You're the only one who needs to see it!"

Susan chuckled at the thought of posting office hours on the door of her home office.

"Okay, if you think it would help, I'll do it. You're the coach."

"That would give you eight plus hours a day for work."

"I'm sure not doing that now."

"Try real office hours for one week. See if you're getting more done in forty hours than you've been accomplishing in sixty."

"Sixty?! God, am I working that many hours?"

"At least. You said you worked nights and weekends."

She agreed. "And if that week works out well, I can opt for another."

"Would you be open to another little time management trick?" I asked.

She was. I told her about structuring her time in twenty-minute segments with five-minute breaks. I reached into my bag and pulled out a copy of my guideline for using a digital timer to take control of time.

"Twenty minutes is a good amount of time to be totally focused, especially when you fight attention deficit disorder." I suggested she clear her workspace of all clocks to help her focus on her work. "During those twenty minutes, don't answer the phone either. Use your voice mail. Change your recording to say 'Thank you for your call, but I'm with a client right now. Leave a message. I return phone calls at 1:00 p.m. and again at 4:30 p.m.'"

"That sounds really business-like!"

"That's the whole idea. Don't interrupt your creative juices while you're working. Return calls later at a set time. You need to be able to accurately bill your time."

"Speaking of not being so accessible to clients, I think I'll stop answering email after hours too."

"Great idea. Answer your emails and voice mail messages no more than three times a day on workdays. Remember you're only working Monday through Friday too. Reply at the beginning of your day, after lunch and before you close up shop at six. You can waste a lot of time answering emails as soon as they appear on your screen. You must limit your distractions in order to get more done. Your clients will get into your routine if you set one."

"What about the mail?"

"Have one basket for personal mail and one for business mail sitting by the front door. Separate your mail at the door. Then walk the mail basket directly to you home office. Only open your business mail in your office during business hours."

"This is sounding pretty rigid."

"It's a temporary approach until you can form better work habits. Try it for three weeks. That's how long it takes to build a new routine."

"What about my client meetings taking so long? What can I do about that?"

"Meet somewhere else more businesslike. What about the library? A public place is all you need. People might get to the point faster if the atmosphere is not so accommodating to conversation. You could even work on your laptop at the library if you wanted to record your meeting notes while they're fresh in your mind."

Susan thought that was a great idea. Less money too.

"I'll do my errands at lunch time or after work like I used to."

"All it takes is self-discipline once you've identified your part in the problem."

Susan added a few more ideas to her list. She even hoped to hire a housekeeper twice a month to help with the housework. The longer the list of changes, the more hopeful Susan looked.

Sometimes all a person needs is time to think. Susan knew what to do to make her life manageable again. She just hadn't taken the time to think things through. Her shrinking income had put her brain into panic mode. She needed an occasion to stop running in circles so she could look at her life objectively. Coaching provided that hour for her. With me sitting beside her, asking the next right question, her thoughts cleared.

Time management was Susan's main problem. Her attention deficit disorder seemed to be a bigger problem at home than it was in her office in town. Susan could also see her part in her financial problem too. She was good at her job and had plenty of clients. She was in no danger of losing business—only losing her free time and her enjoyment of life.

Managing time is a common problem for creative people. Susan's decision to work out of her home removed structure and accountability from her day. When she had peers working around her, she was more productive. Someone else set the work ethic standard and Susan met it. Working out of her house made it easy to take time to vacuum dog hair instead of meeting deadlines. Meeting clients at the coffee shop gave her an excuse to attach errands to the end of her meetings. She simply was not putting in enough billable hours, even though she was working days, nights and weekends. Activity does not necessarily mean productivity. Susan needed more structure. She would have to enforce some new rules to get her business back in order.

Susan redirected the conversation, "I want to talk about art now, not commercial art, my art."

"Okay, what do you want to create?"

With a smile on her face she pulled a large coffee table sized book out of her backpack. "Look here," she pointed to the cover artwork, "This artist does mixed media pieces using text and photocopied images. I really like his stuff."

I took a moment to flip through the pages. "These are really interesting. I can see why you like them."

She pointed thoughtfully at a beautifully complicated image in the book and looked straight at me, "I want to make art like this."

"What's keeping you from doing that?"

She looked puzzled for a split second then her face brightened, "I don't guess anything at all! I don't work evenings or weekends!"

I waved to our waitress and paid the check.

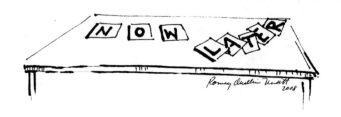

Now and Later

An enthusiastic group of writers gathered in a cavernous meeting room at the public library. With the front rows filled, the group was anxious to start. I only had an hour to speak.

"I need a volunteer from the group." A few writers looked up, interested, but not quite willing to volunteer. Others looked down, avoiding eye contact, concentrating on the meeting agenda. No takers. I rephrased my question, "Does anyone here have the very enviable problem of having too many ideas and you can't decide which to start first?" A woman raised her hand high and smiled.

"Having the ability to generate ideas is one of the blessings of a creative mind. Having trouble choosing between these ideas is one of the curses!" I leaned across a couple seated at the end of her row and read her nametag, "Genevieve, thanks for volunteering." She was ready to play.

"Please write down one idea on each sheet of paper." I handed her a small yellow notepad. "In a few minutes I'll ask you to come up and play a game with me." She started writing.

"Genevieve has more ideas than she knows what to do with. Some of you here today are stuck and can't think of a thing to write." I believe if I handed each of you ten slips of paper and a pen and told you to go off to a quiet spot to think for fifteen minutes, you could come back to your seat with at least ten ideas, maybe even twenty. Sometimes we just need to get quiet on the inside so we can hear our inner coach's coaching."

The group was interested now. "Too many ideas or no ideas at all can keep you from working. Either way, too many or too few ideas cause anxiety. This game will help cut through the mental clutter." By this time Genevieve had a stack of yellow papers in her hands.

"Genevieve, let's play the 'Now and Later Game.' Come up to the table." She sprang out of her seat and with a playful gait walked to the table. I reached out for her stack of papers.

"Tell me, what do you write?"

"I write articles and short stories for children's magazines."

"I loved *Highlights* magazine," I said, "Especially the hidden picture puzzle at the back."

I held up each of the ten sheets of paper as I counted them aloud. "Looks like there's no creative block here." Genevieve smiled at my acknowledgement of her creativity.

I arranged the small yellow squares on the table side by side in a long row. The words written on each sheet faced Genevieve.

I addressed the group, "For this decision making game, I don't need to read what's on these pieces of paper, Genevieve knows and that's all that matters."

I explained the process. "Genevieve is going to help me demonstrate an intuitive decision making strategy. Some of you may remember a hard chewy nougat candy called 'Now and Later.' Like that sticky candy, sometimes creative people get stuck—chewing and chewing, trying to choose one idea over another. You can overanalyze an idea or think it to death. When you can't make a decision, this game might help you get going again. I designed the 'Now and Later Game' to help my coaching clients learn to trust their intuition."

"No matter how many ideas you have, you can categorize your ideas into two basic groups— *now* ideas and *later* ideas. This is a neutral distinction. Most people make the mistake of dividing their ideas into other less helpful groups such as good ideas and bad ideas. Can anyone share any other ways you've evaluated your ideas?"

A man towards the back said, "I try to figure out which ideas will sell and which won't."

"Judging an idea strictly on market value may cut your creativity short," I said. "Who really knows what idea will sell?

Interesting articles are printed on not-so-interesting topics every day."

"A woman dressed in a flowing skirt and Birkenstocks said, "If I find out someone else has published an article on a topic I've been considering, I automatically throw that one out."

"So you're always trying to find a totally new idea."

"Yes, and it's exhausting."

"I can only imagine!"

"Let's just be honest. Most of us think too much." The group of writers chuckled. "With too much thinking and judging, you can kill any idea. Don't rush to judgment on your ideas. Let them be. What sounds like a bad idea today may be the perfect idea tomorrow. So what if someone else has recently written on an idea? That may mean the topic is hot and your idea would sell. Give yourself the permission to keep all of your ideas. This game takes the left-brain, the thinking side of your brain out of your decision making process and allows your right-brain, intuitive side to come front and center."

I turned my attention to Genevieve, "Let me explain how the game works. A *now* idea is an idea you could start on immediately. You know enough to begin today. You have the right materials or information at hand. A *later* idea requires more research, time or resources than you have available today."

"Genevieve, please sort your ideas into two rows, a row of nows and a row of laters."

With hardly a moment's hesitation, the trail of yellow papers shifted into two lines.

"Please pull out your laters." She handed the papers to me. "You may want to use these ideas some other time. As long as you have the ideas recorded, you don't have to waste any of your mental energy trying to remember them. Put these in a drawer or file and keep these for later. The four left on the table are your nows?" She nodded. "Please look at the four pieces of paper. Make sure you're familiar with each idea."

She looked at the four sheets of paper for a moment.

"Now close your eyes and take a deep breath." She took a deep breath and exhaled.

"Take one more breath and then open your eyes." Some in the room decided to take in some extra oxygen too.

On the exhale, she opened her eyes and a smile came on her face. She looked as if she were expecting a surprise.

"Which of these ideas is calling you to action right now?"

She picked up one piece of paper and handed it to me. I read it aloud, "Spooky stories from America's past."

The audiences clapped as if they had witnessed a magician doing a card trick.

"Do you feel ready to write this today?" I asked Genevieve.

"Yes, I do!" She returned to her seat.

"Now what questions do you have?" I asked the group.

One of the writers raised her hand, "Why take the time to write the ideas down on a piece of paper? Couldn't we sort through the ideas in our heads?"

"When you write your ideas down, they become real. Real ideas get more action than never-recorded ideas. Never-recorded ideas are easily forgotten."

The lady in the comfortable shoes raised her hand, "Wouldn't a list work just as well? Why take the time to rewrite the ideas on separate pieces of paper?"

"A list is static. When you make a list, you probably write what you think is most important at the top and write the less important things at the bottom. Then you try to work your way down the page. That's a reasonable way to tackle errands, but not creative ideas. When each idea is written on a separate piece of paper, each idea can be considered independently. When each idea is given its own piece of paper, every idea is given equal weight and value."

"I have a question for Genevieve," the man interested in selling looked at Genevieve, "How did you know which idea to choose?"

She thought for a moment, "I don't really know how I knew, I just knew. When I opened my eyes after taking a deep breath, that one paper caught my eye. That was the one that seemed right."

The man looked skeptical, "Does it still feel right?"

"Yes, it does. I'm anxious to start."

"How else could this game work?" he asked.

I brainstormed for a moment, "Let's say you have a new book. To promote your book you need to have several book signings. You've generated a list of possible venues—libraries and bookstores in several neighboring communities. You need to make contact with someone at each place to see if they'd be willing to host you, but you hate to ask strangers for favors. You put off making the calls."

A few people nodded in agreement.

"Couldn't the 'Now and Later Game' help move you to action? Put each name or place for a book signing on a separate piece of paper. Spread your papers out on the table and move them around. The kinetic action of moving papers around seems to help people make a decision. Look at your papers. See if some of your choices seem like nows and let others be laters. Then narrow it down to one. Isn't it possible that the choice you make could've been prompted by your intuition? What if you made the phone call to the bookstore right away? What if that person wasn't busy and had the time to talk to you? How could it hurt to try a new strategy? This game is at least a novel way to move you to take action on an unpleasant task. "

My "Now and Later Game" employs intuition. I believe if a person can formulate a question, they already know the answer. Our inner wisdom knows what we are ready for, what we have the energy or enthusiasm to do. This inner knowing comes from the creative side of our brain. If Genevieve played the game tomorrow, she might choose another idea. The decision one makes is subjective. Inner intuition and how it works is one of the mysteries of creativity.

"Someday" Never Comes

"This is a workshop on how to combat procrastination," I looked at the digital clock on the wall, "So, I'll start on time. The procrastinators will be here shortly.

"Perfectionists?" A few teachers looked up and waved. I smiled as I held up a stack of printed class notes, "Here are the notes from this workshop. I know you would like to have these now, but I'll keep them until the end of the workshop so you won't have a chance to read ahead."

The educators were relaxed, fresh from a leisurely lunch, enjoying a day away from regular classroom responsibilities.

"Both procrastination and perfectionism limit your productivity and steal your inner sense of control. Both procrastination and perfectionism can cause major and minor inconveniences in your life. You miss the beginning of a movie, don't get your bills paid on time or never get around to going for that check-up." I walked in between the tables in the classroom. "We postpone all kinds of important and not-so-important tasks in our lives. Some people even postpone doing the thing in life they love to do, such as writing or painting, taking a walk with a friend or buying strawberries when they're in season."

About this time a few stragglers come in the room. I motioned them toward the empty seats at the front of the room.

"Procrastination and perfectionism are two sides of the same coin. Both of these habits of behavior will keep you from reaching your goals. We're here today to find six ways to combat these two thieves of time. The goal is to make time for creative and leisure activities that will enrich our enjoyment of life."

"What kinds of creative things do you wish you had time to do?" I asked. With a dry erase marker I recorded their comments: writing a family history, leading a retreat for church, learning to play the piano, painting watercolors, tango dancing, gardening.

"What about practical things you wish you had time to do?"

"Pay my bills on time."

"Get the garage cleared out so I can park my car in it."

"Keep better records for tax time."

"Exercise for better health."

I stood at the front of the room, "Goals, whether creative or practical, are easily derailed by someday thinking," I wrote 'Someday' on the board.

"Someday thinking is a trap that will keep you from living the life you say you want to live. So when is someday?"

"Someday is when I lose twenty pounds!" the P.E. coach said.

"How about thirty?" a woman on the back row added.

"Someday is when my kids are gone," a young woman said.

"Someday is when I've retired," said the school secretary.

"You're getting the idea." I said. "Someday is whenever you'll finally get around to it, whatever "it" may be. Someday is when all conditions are right, when your calendar is completely clear, when the planets are perfectly aligned."

I leaned forward as if to tell a secret and whispered, "Someday *never* comes. Someday will cheat you out of your dreams for a more fulfilling life. Someday thinking will kill a dream one excuse at a time."

Someone's cell phone rang breaking the concentration. I paused while the special education teacher rushed out of the room to answer her call.

"Putting off doing things will always have a consequence."

I wrote "Consequences" on the board.

"What are some of the consequences of inaction due to either procrastination or perfectionism?"

"Credit card late fees," one young teacher suggested. Several groaned loudly in agreement.

"No one to help me do the job because I waited until the last minute to start," another added.

"Doing less than my best because of lack of time."

"Debt."

"Frustration."

"Clutter."

"Broken trust."

I wrote several of their answers on the board.

"What are some of the emotional consequences when we suffer due to procrastination and perfectionism?"

"Feeling ashamed."

"Disappointing others."

"Anxiety."

"Worry."

"Headaches."

I looked at the long list of words covering the board.

"All these consequences you've named seem to me to be pretty compelling reasons to not fall into procrastination and perfectionism. Many of us clearly are perfectionists and procrastinators and so are many of our students. We all struggle with taking action in a timely fashion."

I moved to sit on the edge of the table at the front of the classroom. "Let's talk about procrastination and perfectionism in the classroom. Why do students put off doing their homework until the last minute?"

A high school teacher shared her opinion, "Many of my students underestimate the scope of the project."

"They're your procrastinators," I said.

"Or they think if they wait to the last minute their parents will have to help them and then they know it will be right," said an elementary teacher.

"They're the perfectionists," I said.

"We're not so different from our students. We underestimated the time it will take to do a project. By the time we'd figured it out, it was too late to ask anyone for help so we pulled an all-nighter. When a task seems especially daunting and we want it to be right, it's easy to put off beginning. We think there's too much at stake if it's not spectacular and amazing. It's also so easy to postpone starting on a project for just one more day, a day that never comes."

"Here's the easy way to remember the difference between procrastination and perfectionism. The Procrastinator says, 'I'll start someday, but not today.' The Perfectionist says, 'When all the conditions are right, I'll start.'"

"Eric Maisel, author of *Coaching the Artist Within*, says we must find a way to create 'in the middle of things'—in the middle of our real, everyday life. Lives full of kids, dogs, traffic jams, illness, bills, repairs and errands. Lives full of negative self-talk, anxiety, worry, and disappointments. Each of us must fight against the interior and exterior challenges that keep us from achieving our goals."

"I think I've just figured something out," a woman seated at the front table blurted out, "I have a project I need and want to do. I want to paint my kitchen cabinets. I thought the reason I haven't started painting the cabinets was because I'm a procrastinator, but that's not true. I haven't started because I'm a perfectionist. I've been promising to paint the cabinets when I have a totally free weekend with no interruptions, no kids at the house and no rain."

"That's classic 'when/then' thinking, very common to perfectionists. When all conditions are right, then I'll do a great job," I said. "I would encourage you to paint a couple of cabinets this Saturday, even if it is raining! Just to get you started. Once you've seen some positive results for your efforts you'll be encouraged to continue."

"If I start the job, my husband might even help me!" she said.

"And even if he doesn't," I smiled, "You'll have the feeling of making progress, which is an empowering feeling."

"Okay, here's your handout." I passed out the sheets, "Let's go over the six steps to combat procrastination and perfectionism."

Here's your copy of the basics of my teacher handout.

Six Steps to Combat Procrastination and Perfectionism

1. **Be present.** Put yourself in the position (literally) to be successful. Remember when you were in school and the teacher called roll? If you were in your seat, you said "Present." Be present in your seat whether that is at your computer, drawing table, or piano bench. Be in your seat or place where things can happen. Be "present." You

can't write a novel while you're mowing the lawn. You can't paint a portrait while you're at the mall.

2.   **Stay**. Once you get to your workspace, stay there. If this feels too awkward after weeks or years of inaction, then set a timer for five minutes or ten minutes or even twenty minutes. Stay in place until the timer goes off. Warning: this may feel like an eternity at the beginning. You won't die or pass out if you feel uncomfortable or self-conscious. The anxious feelings will pass. Breathe. Try to relax.

Put your fingers on the keyboard, they'll eventually start twitching. Pick up your drawing pencil and doodle. Strum your guitar strings. If you're too scared to begin a new project, just stay in place until the timer goes off. Give yourself a chance to be in the place where creativity could bubble up. Your mind will appreciate a few minutes to mull over the possibility of creating again.

Now here's the important part, while the timer is keeping track of time, don't leave your workspace. Stay. Do not move—not for a phone call, not for a pet, not for a forgotten commitment. The world will still be in place after the timer goes off. After your twenty minutes you can take care of whatever it was that tried to kidnap your creative focus. Give yourself the gift of time. Time spent in the right physical space is a powerful beginning.

3.   **Don't look back.** While you're in your workspace spending time, do not think about all the reasons why you've not been doing what you said you wanted to do. If you want to paint, it doesn't matter if you haven't painted for twenty years. If you want to write, it doesn't matter if you haven't written in your journal for two years. It simply does not matter! Don't complain, justify, or feel regret for the lost years. Administer your own absolution. Forgive yourself for your pattern of inaction and start anew. That was then, this is now, and now is a great time to begin.

4.   **Believe in the power of "good enough."** Wanting the right time and place to begin again is understandable but waiting for what will never be a reality is a waste of time.

Know that creative people, just like accountants, mothers, sanitation workers, and schoolteachers all do their jobs in less than perfect conditions. There is no perfect world but most days the world is a "good enough" place to be. Decide that a "good enough" work environment is okay for today. Your painting corner doesn't have to be outfitted like a professional's studio in order for you to begin painting. Your office doesn't have to pass inspection for you to write the Great American Novel. Fifteen minutes of practice three times a week is better than none. Conditions do not have to be right for you to begin; just beginning will create those right conditions.

5. **Take action and don't stop.** Write one word, one sentence, squirt out your paints, or put your hands on the keyboard. Move in the direction of your dreams. Start and don't stop. Do something! Don't show your work to other people. Keep your creative work your little secret. You don't have to create perfection today, you just need to create something you've never done before.

6. **Today!** Today is always the best possible day to begin, don't wait for Someday.

When the Student is Ready
the Teacher Will Appear

In 1998 I was considering enrolling in seminary. I made an appointment with a minister friend of mine. I brought a long list of carefully prepared reasons why seminary was not a good idea.

"I already have one master's degree. What do I need with another one?"

He nodded.

"If I'm not going to be a minister, why would I go to seminary?"

He shrugged his shoulders.

"The tuition is so high!"

He agreed.

"I would have to quit my job as a high school art teacher."

He tipped his head downward and looked at me over the top of his glasses. Now I knew that *everyone* knew how much I hated teaching high school students.

"Okay," I said, "quitting teaching is actually on the 'pro' side of my pro and con list."

He smiled slightly.

I continued. "In seminary you have to write papers all the time. I'm an artist, I don't know how to write *papers*!"

"You write well enough."

In desperation I raised my voice, "I don't have any *real* reason to go to seminary, except..." I stopped to reconsider what I was about to say.

"Except what?" he asked before I could complete my mental editing.

"Except that it is the desire of my heart." I looked up at him searching for approval.

He nodded.

After a quiet moment he leaned toward me across his big desktop and said, "Romney, when the student is ready, the teacher will appear."

Guess who my teacher was that day?

I went to seminary.

I wrote papers.

I became a minister.

Since that visit with my favorite theological mentor, I've heard his wise statement repeated many times—maybe not in the exactly the same words, but with the same meaning. It's true. When the student is ready, the teacher will appear.

Thinking back on my life I've been blessed with the right teacher at the right time over and over again, always at the perfect moment when I was ready to learn something important about life.

I grew up in the 1960's in Bethany, Oklahoma. It was a time long before cable television, twenty-four hour cartoon stations or video games. To pass the summer afternoons I filled the time with a variety of creative pursuits.

I practiced drawing with Jon Gnagy, a beatnik looking artist who had a drawing show on television. My official Jon Gnagy Art Kit contained charcoal pencils, sandpaper for sharpening charcoal sticks, paper and a how-to-draw book. I learned how to draw a covered bridge, cowboy on a bucking bronco and a house down a winding road with a mailbox perilously close to the viewer to emphasis the magic of perspective.

The majority of my summer was spent writing scripts for our neighborhood productions of fairy tales. Our street was unpaved and sparsely populated with children. Available cast members were the Perry kids next door, Theresa, Randy and Carla, the Bazemore children across the street, Barbara, Billy and Bobby and my sister, Felecia.

Theresa Perry was just enough older than the rest of us to decline being roped into my productions. Her brother, Randy, who was my age, was hard to pin down too, as his reason for living was to search and destroy ants, blowing up their hills with Black Cat firecrackers. When duty called, being the only boy old enough to read, he was always the prince. Randy's prince costume consisted of a baby blanket tied around his neck and cowboy boots.

My sister Felecia with her thick braid of strawberry blond hair was a natural for Rapunzel looking down from a painted cardboard castle window. If a witch was needed to hold out an apple for Snow White, as director I made a Hitchcock-esque cameo appearance for the thrill of an out-of-season reason to wear one of my Halloween costumes.

After many days of secret rehearsals held behind a curtain made of two quilts pinned to the clothesline, the cast made tickets and sold them door to door. Our parents and neighbors paid twenty-five cents for their tickets and fifty cents for a bag of Jiffy Pop popcorn and a Dixie cup of lemonade. The adults brought lawn chairs and sat in rows in our back yard theatre and applauded wildly at the end of every scene.

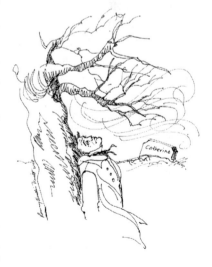

In between producing plays I read. Every couple of days I rode my aqua blue Schwinn to refresh my supply of Nancy Drew mysteries from the Bethany Library. When I began rereading my favorite *The Secret*

of the Old Clock my mother noticed and she had a little talk with me.

"Romney, you're such a good reader. There are so many other wonderful stories to read." She handed me her copies of *Jane Eyre* and *Wuthering Heights*. Ah ha! Nancy Drew could not hold a candle to the dangerous charms of Heathcliff and Mr.Rochester!

In the fall of my fourth grade year I did a book report on *Rebecca* by Daphne duMaurier. If you haven't read *Rebecca* then you've missed one of the most beautiful first lines of any novel: "Last night I dreamt I went to Manderley again."

My oral book report ended with this standard fourth grade line: "If you want to know what happened then you'll have to read the book yourself."

The teacher quizzed me. "What did you say was the main character's name?"

"Mrs. Maxim de Winter," I said.

"No, what was her *first* name?"

"No one ever said. She was only called Mrs. de Winter."

"You must not have read the book. Her name had to be Rebecca." She told me to take my seat and handed me my book report with a red grading pencil "C" scribbled at the top. I was insulted and embarrassed.

That afternoon I showed my mother my grade and told her the whole story. To make sure she understood the severity of my public reprimand I said, "My teacher is as mean as Mrs. Danvers!" My mother gasped. Mrs. Danvers was the sinister housekeeper and loyal friend of the late Mrs. Rebecca de Winter.

My mother rushed to my defense and called the teacher. She accused her of being an uneducated literary imbecile who had no business teaching school. She also informed the teacher Mrs. de Winter was the only name given for the second wife of Mr. Maxim de Winter.

My mother found the perfect teachable moment and seized it. She pushed me to read just past my ability and introduced me to the magic of literature. When the student is ready, the teacher will appear.

♦♦♦

As a ten-year-old girl growing up in a Baptist church in Oklahoma City, I loved Sunday School. Our department director was an old man who loved the stories of the Bible but couldn't tell a story to save his life.

Once in a while our class was saved from his monotone stories by Mrs. McCartney's quiet entrance into the back of our classroom. She opened the door and stood behind waiting to be invited in. Our invitation was a collective and gleeful "Mrs. McCartney!"

It was the opinion of nine-to-twelve-year-olds at our church that Mrs. McCartney was the best storyteller in the world. When she told a Bible story, children listened. It was as if she had been there—wherever *there* was. Whether on the wilderness plains with the Israelites complaining about manna or watching Elijah being taken up into the heavens in the chariot of fire, Mrs. McCartney knew her stuff. We were convinced she knew everything and everybody.

Mrs. McCartney had another talent besides storytelling. She was an artist. In the evening service on Easter Sunday she did a chalk talk. Her easel was set up next to the pulpit with a large piece of white paper stapled to a board. After hymn singing and prayers the lights were turned low. Mrs. McCartney walked up the three chancel steps to stand in front of her easel.

She delivered an Easter sermon in line and color. In her own special way full of drama and detail she told the story of Jesus' crucifixion and death. In chalk she sketched a lonely hill and an orange and yellow sunset. In black chalk she drew three black crosses silhouetted against the sky.

She spoke softly, "His friends laid his body in a borrowed tomb." A round-mouthed chalk cave emerged from the side of a hill below the three crosses.

"A stone was rolled in front of the opening." She drew a large round gray rock in front of the opening of the tomb.

"The next morning the women came to prepare his body for burial. A great earthquake shook the earth and an angel of the Lord came and rolled the stone away and sat on it." She drew the stone toppled over and an angel with white wings perched on the stone.

"The angel said to the women, 'Do not be afraid. I know you are looking for Jesus who was crucified.'" She took a breath and paused. I held my breath.

In a loud clear voice she said slowly, "'He is not here; for HE IS RISEN!'"

I gasped. Goosebumps appeared on my arms.

With a stick of chalk she drew bright beams of yellow light streaming from the empty tomb.

"On this day, Easter Sunday, we celebrate the resurrection of our Lord, Jesus Christ." She turned and walked down the stairs and sat on the front row.

I exhaled. In awe I turned to my mother sitting next to me on the pew and whispered, "When I grow up I want to be just like Mrs. McCartney."

And I did try to do that very thing.

Mrs. McCartney was one of my earliest teachers and I was her ready and able student of the arts. I paid attention to the way she used the chalks to lay in wide areas of soft color. I listened carefully to the way she told a story. Mrs. McCartney taught me that my artistic talents could be used to draw attention to the things that really mattered. And she taught me the value of a story well told.

When the student is ready, the teacher will appear.

Another teacher appeared my freshman year in college. Mr. George Tutt was chairman of the art department at William Woods College. He taught Watercolor I during Short Term in the spring semester. Short Term was a four-week class. For one month, just before the end of the school year, students took a class from nine a.m. to noon every day. After class you were free to enjoy the Missouri spring days and do your homework, of course. Most students took easy classes and planned to spend their afternoons working on their tans and their evenings with their boyfriends.

On the first day of class we were expected to have our supplies. I'd purchased nearly one hundred dollars worth of art supplies for this class. When I called home to get more money put in my bank account to cover my charge at the college bookstore my truck-driver daddy had a fit. He thought it was ridiculous to spend twenty-five dollars on a paintbrush. He expressed his disbelief with his favorite line, "What do you think I am? Made out of money?!" Of course, that was exactly what I thought, but I had the good sense to keep my mouth shut.

I arrived at class early, carrying my yellow tackle box of watercolor supplies. I took a seat at a long table and proudly arranged my tube watercolor paints, expensive camel hair brushes, and watercolor paper.

Mr. Tutt opened the door to the classroom. He stopped his body a dark silhouette backlit by blinding sunlight from a nearby window. He looked like a rock star.

In a gruff voice he ordered "Girls, take out a pencil and a piece of watercolor paper." We obeyed. "Draw a horizontal line across that piece of paper."

"Where do you want us to draw the line?" a brave soul asked.

"Just draw a line," he said.

Another tried to get more information, "Mr. Tutt, do you want us to draw the line high or low on the page?"

"Just draw a line," he said turning away from the sound of her voice.

"Do you want the paper vertical or horizontal?"

No answer, just an exasperated sigh.

We were all trying so hard to please him.

Slowly and with a bit of irritation he raised his voice and said one more time, "Just draw a line on the piece of paper."

I chose a horizontal format, picked up my pencil and drew a line about one inch from the bottom of the piece of paper from the left side of the paper all the way across to the right. I set my pencil down.

Mr. Tutt sauntered around the room eyeing everyone's lines suspiciously. He walked to my table and tapped my paper, "Romney, are you from Kansas, Oklahoma or Texas?"

"Oklahoma?" I said as if I wasn't entirely sure.

"That's what I thought," he said and walked away.

How could he have known? I was sure this man was more amazing than The Amazing Kreskin.

After a few minutes of show-stopping mind reading with other students he revealed his secret.

"When I told you to draw a line on your piece of paper, you drew a horizon line, the line where the sky meets the ground. Some of you drew your line close to the bottom of the page because you're from plains states, big sky country. Others of you drew your line high on the page because you're from mountainous areas of the country—more ground, less sky."

Even though his logical explanation for his mind reading ability made all kinds of sense, I was still amazed.

He began to walk slowly in between the tables making quick eye contact with each of us much like a prison warden inspecting his new inmates.

"Now, listen up." He waited until we were all giving him our full attention.

"Watercolor is a Short Term class. Lots of students at this college think Short Term is when they're supposed to sunbathe on the roof of the sorority house and run around with fraternity boys in convertibles."

I was right all along. He *was* a mind reader.

He walked to the chalkboard at the front of the room. "If you think that's what you're going to be doing, you're wrong! You don't have time to work on your tan or ride around in cars with boys because you're going to be painting *every day*." He eyed the crowd to make sure we believed him.

"You know why you're going to be painting? Because this is watercolor class and the only way you can learn how to paint watercolors is to paint lots of watercolors."

He took a piece of chalk and wrote the number "60" on the board. He slammed his chalk at the number. "This is the number of watercolors you're going to paint between today and the last day of this class four weeks from now."

I leaned back in my chair, my mouth open in disbelief.

"That means every Friday you're going to turn in fifteen paintings." He wrote the number fifteen on the board, "Fifteen watercolors every Friday." Tapping his chalk with each syllable he continued, "Fif-teen-times-four-is-six-ty." He tapped his chalk on the board one more time for emphasis and turned to look our way. "Now let's get started."

That was day one. He was right; I painted afternoons and evenings and late into the night. I learned to paint by painting every day.

This capable teacher put a demand on my potential as a student artist. He set the bar high and I jumped over it. He taught me to do more work than everyone else was doing, and when you do more, you get more. That spring I learned to paint and best of all, I fell in love with the medium of watercolor. Mr. Tutt came into my life at a time when I was ready to learn. A few years later I earned a master's degree in watercolor painting. Now as a teacher I sometimes use his old "horizon-line trick" to amaze my art students. I'd like them to think I can read their minds.

When the student is ready, the teacher will appear.

Some years later in my mid-twenties, a woman at my church saw leadership potential in me. For the most part since my Mrs. McCartney days I had been the unofficial minister of all-things-art at church—bulletin covers, backdrops for_ cantatas, T-shirts designs etc.

My soon-to-be-mentor was a popular Bible study leader in our church. One Sunday morning in her business-like manner of speaking she said to me, "You have leadership skills that need to be used. I intend to nominate you to be the President of the Day Baptist Women. Will you accept?"

I agreed to be on the slate, was elected due to her stamp of approval and I began my mentorship with her. Watching her in action I learned how to speak to persuade. Assisting her at conferences, I saw how to prepare a workshop that would lead people to new insights. Skills I learned from her have come in handy when I speak in public.

This woman, the age of my mother, spotted me as a ready student and she presented herself to me as my teacher, if I cared to learn what she knew best. All I had to do was tag along and take notes. When the student is ready, the right teacher will notice!

The first line from *The Road Less Traveled* by M. Scott Peck summed up life in my forties, "Life is difficult."

I was really tired of myself. For years I'd tried to push everyone and everything into place so the world would run on my schedule. I was of the opinion that if everyone would do their part (on time and to my satisfaction) life would be so much easier—especially for me. My way was the highway, until my own efforts created the dead end I needed to turn around a go a different way.

Not only did I struggle with the outside world, I struggled with my inner creative spirit. I was in the middle years of what would stretch out to be an eleven-year creative drought in which I found no joy in my art. I could paint and draw but my passion for being an artist had disappeared. This was a profound loss, I felt flat.

I wanted to live my life in a new way but I didn't know how. I called my counselor desperate for an appointment. The only time he had available was 8:00 a.m. on Christmas Eve. I'm sure he would have rather slept in. I arrived early, rushed in and sat on the coach, anxious to begin.

"I'm so tired. I don't want to be a warrior any more. I want to learn how to be a magician."

"What would that mean for you to live life as a magician?" He always asks the next right question.

I thought for a moment. "Living life with a magician's view of the world would mean I could accept change and deal with it with grace and peace. I could relax, go with the flow, and stop fighting my way upstream every day."

"Do you know anyone who is living the kind of life you want to live?"

"No, mostly I just read about this way of living in books, but," I thought for a moment, "I can think of one woman my age and a couple of others who might be living the life I want."

"How do you think someone learns how to live life as a magician?" he asked.

"Probably through life experience, struggle, and disappointment," I said. Things I knew pretty well. "They might have had a mentor too, someone who took them under their wing."

"Until you find someone who'll do that for you, continue to read whatever you're reading, for now, these authors are your mentors. As you have opportunity, watch these women and listen to what they say. Notice how they live life, how they view problems. Learn from them. I have every confidence you can make this shift. You're already well on your way."

I left his office feeling hopeful, free to make a change in my life. It was a wonderful Christmas present. My feeling of freedom came from the realization I'd crossed some long emotional rope bridge spanning a chasm over choppy water. One side of the gap was where I had been, the other side the opening to new places I would go. Standing on the edge I looked back and watched the bridge fall away. Once you cross the bridge that leads you to your next phase of life, you can't go back. You can't pretend you don't know what you know.

I followed my counselor's advice. I began to say "No" to more opportunities to be in charge. Now the thought of chairing a committee drained me. I needed all my time and energy to restore my inner spirit which by this point was as dry as an empty well. I had to rethink my habits and patterns of response in order to find a way to live life on peaceful terms, unattached to the outcome. I yearned for a sense of willing acceptance of whatever came my way. I couldn't fight life anymore; I wanted to live in the predictable chaos of everyday with grace and love. I needed a teacher.

When I met Sue Preece I could see that she had what I was looking for—serenity. When we had a chance to talk I confessed, "I used to think I knew what was best for me and for everyone else, but I don't have a clue. If I don't know what's best for me, who does?"

"God," Sue said the answer to that question and all other questions was simply "God."

Here are some of the many things I've learned from Sue, the magician. She said when she was a willing student she learned these things from her teacher/mentor. When I was ready to learn, Sue passed them on to me. She's still my teacher, I'm still her student and now we're friends.

Sue's Clues

1. Live life on a need-to-know basis with God, when you need to know, God will let you know.

2. Memorize The Serenity Prayer. "God grant me the serenity to accept the things I cannot change, the courage to change the things I can, and wisdom to know the difference." The only person you can change is you—your thoughts, actions and attitudes. You can't change anybody else.

3. There are at least seven solutions to every problem so don't think you've found the perfect solution. That's because…

4. God always has a Plan A and Plan B, C, etc. Say "This or something better God." This or something better means "I'm open to all the goodness and abundance you have in mind for me, God. Bring it on!"

5. When a problem arises, don't dwell on what the other person said or did. Look at the situation and honestly ask "What's my part in this problem?"

6. Mind your own business. Other people have the right to live their own lives in whatever way they choose. They get to make their own mistakes too.

7. Keep your own side of the street clean. Do the next right thing you know to do. If you mess up, make amends.

8. When you have a problem, ask God to show you the next right step. When the next right step appears take it. Don't expect a dissertation from God; expect Map-Quest style directions that come in one line at a time. Example: "Go 2.5 miles, turn left, and continue." That's enough to get you going in the right direction.

9. Live and let live. Most people are honestly doing the best they know how. When they understand a little more, they'll do a little better. We're all God's works in progress.

10. If you hear a person say "I know" that means the person isn't willing to learn something new. Example: "I know my chances of winning the lottery are slim but I only

spend fifty dollars a week on tickets." This person has decided they have their answer.

11.   A "Yes, but," means he or she can't listen and has a closed mind. Example: "Yes, but I'm so sure this is the right man for me. He said he'll leave his wife just as soon she's conquered her fear of spiders." This person will probably continue their present course for a while longer.

12.   An "If only" statement means he or she is not operating in reality. Example: "If only my mother hadn't let me stop taking piano lessons I would have become a famous concert soloist." This is similar to the "When/then" statements common to perfectionists such as, "When my house is clean, then I'll start writing." This person is living in some yet-to-be-discovered parallel universe where things are always "better."

13.   A "What if?" response such as "What if I change jobs and it doesn't work out?" means he or she is not ready (or too afraid) to take action on their own behalf. A "What if?" statement means this person is hoping someone else will swoop in like Zorro and solve the problem.

14.   Make plans, but don't plan the outcome.

15.   Never use an ink pen to write something in your calendar. Plans change, things come up, use a pencil, save yourself some aggravation.

16.   You can change your plans. If you've over-packed your day you can call your friend or your dentist and say "Something's come up and I need to reschedule." That person probably wrote your name on their calendar in pencil.

17.   Acceptance is the answer to all your problems. Act as if everything that happens today is exactly as it should be.

18.   Don't waste your time asking God "Why me?" instead ask, "What do I do now?" Release your need for some cosmic explanation for everything that happens to you— it's not coming. Be willing to trust that there's a bigger picture.

19.   Everything's temporary. Jobs, relationships, the weather and your feelings.
20.   Everything's not your fault. There are other people in the world that contribute to the chaos.
21.   The less you know about what your teenager is doing, the happier you'll be.
22.   It's more fun to be happy than to be right.
23.   God is never late.
24.   Don't go to the hardware store looking for bread.

When I was ready to be a student, Sue taught me from her magic book of wisdom.

The mentor who is most prominent in my life these days is my writing teacher and colleague, Peggy Fielding. I began writing to fend off my nervous energy.

I've been in school off and on my whole lifetime. The most challenging time was my four and a half years in seminary. Seminary is school on steroids. You read what other people tell you to read and write about what they tell you to read and then you do it all over again the next week until you finally graduate, then you write sermons every week. Write, write, and write.

When my seminary career was over I didn't know what to do with myself. My life had been highly regimented for thirteen semesters and in three weeks time I'd turned in the last paper and been ordained. I felt as if I'd been thrown off a speeding train. My mind was still racing and I didn't have a single assignment to complete. Like an addict I went back to the only thing I knew that would calm me—school. I needed class, a teacher, and an assignment and I needed it right now!

I enrolled in a writing class at my local community college. The name "Fielding" was listed beside almost every one of the writing classes in the non-credit catalog. The first class I took from Peggy was on how to make a living as a writer. The second class I took from her was on non-fiction writing. The third class was on writing confession stories. The fourth class was called "Ninety-Nine Ways to Make a Living as a Writer" or something like that. The fifth class was "Query, Synopsis and Proposal." I've lost track of what came next, but I'm waiting for the next time she offers a class on writing romance. She's an excellent teacher and I am her perpetual ready student.

Peggy is a remarkable woman. Her life stories are entertaining and she tells them to make a point about writing. The first night of class she gives her homework assignment: set up your writing area, get a copy of *The Elements of Style, Writer's Market,* a dictionary, a copy of the King James Version of the Bible (so you'll know what beautiful language sounds like), decide on a time to write every day and most importantly—write every day for twenty minutes. No exceptions she said, "Unless you have special dispensation from the Pope or the President of the Southern Baptist Convention."

The next class she asked every person "Where is your writing space? When is your writing time? Did you write every day without fail for twenty minutes?"

There is no way you can lie to this woman. She has the cool glare of a seasoned schoolteacher who can spot a faker. Everyone sings as if they'd been injected with a truth serum. At the end of the second class she ups the writing time to thirty minutes a day. The third class the time goes up to forty-five minutes a day. The next class she expects an hour a day. After that, you're either writing and loving it or you've dropped out of the class due to your inability to stand the heat in Peggy's kitchen.

With her push in the right direction I queried *Art Focus Oklahoma Magazine* and offered my services as a writer in their "Business of Art" section. I proposed a new column, "Ask a Creativity Coach" and sent a three-hundred-word sample in to the editor. In a few minutes I received an email response requesting a column for every issue. Success!

Peggy gave me courage to write what I knew and send it in! You can't win unless you enter and you can't get published unless you write and send it in. She makes it sound so simple, but I've found out it's very hard to write one word after another. Even taking my own advice as a creativity coach and putting my butt in the chair and my fingers on the keyboard every day for a lot longer than an hour a day, there have been times when I've been overcome with fear and anxiety. "What do I think I'm doing?!" Other times I feel so nervous and uncomfortable I eat handfuls of licorice jellybeans until I'm sick. Writing is hard work, but some days are easier than others.

Like the woman at my church who could see my leadership potential, Peggy asks me to help with her book signings and do the introducing when she and her colleagues speak. Acting as a gatekeeper she's also recommended me for various positions on committees and given me writing leads. As her willing student, I'm thankful for the opportunities to expand my writing circle of influence. She's a good friend.

Peggy's as demanding as my watercolor teacher, Mr. Tutt. He taught me the importance of painting every day; Peggy taught me the importance of writing every day. Both George Tutt and Peggy Fielding taught me the secret to being a professional: sit in your chair and do your work every day.

Peggy knows the writing business and I'm happy to be one of her protégés. This book would not have been written without her encouragement and mentoring, for that, I am so thankful. When the student is ready, the teacher will appear.

About the Author and Illustrator

Romney Oualline Nesbitt, creativity coach, artist, public school art teacher, writer and ordained minister in the Christian Church (Disciples of Christ) helps writers and artists move past perceived limitations to reach their creative goals.

Nesbitt has a B.F.A. in art from William Woods University, Fulton, Missouri, a Master of Art in painting from The University of Tulsa and a Master of Divinity from Phillips Theological Seminary. Nesbitt has been a minister since 2000.

Nesbitt is President of the Tulsa NightWriters, a member of Oklahoma Writer's Federation, Inc., Oklahoma Visual Arts Coalition, Creativity Coaching Association, and Spiritual Directors International.

The author teaches a series of classes on living the creative life for Tulsa Community College, writes a coaching column for *Art Focus Oklahoma Magazine* titled "Ask a Creativity Coach" and articles on the business of art. She is a popular speaker and workshop leader on the subject of creativity.

She has used her artistic talents as a courtroom artist, commercial artist, book illustrator and fine artist and teacher. On a mission trip to Niger, Africa in 1997 she drew pencil portraits of witchdoctors, imams and villagers. She teaches art and creative thinking skills to her fifth and sixth grade students at Jenks West Intermediate School in Jenks, Oklahoma.

More Secrets!

Discussion questions for each chapter are posted on my
website, www.romneynesbitt.com.

For my readers who would like to explore the ideas presented
in this book in greater detail, I've written discussion questions to
accompany each chapter in the book. *Secrets from a Creativity
Coach Workbook* is on line and absolutely free. Just log onto my
website www.romneynesbitt.com and click the link for this book,
Secrets from a Creativity Coach. Answer the questions on your
own or form a book study group with your friends and answer the
questions together. Putting pen to paper will push your thinking a
little deeper and encourage you to take action.

My website has lots of other information about my creativity
coaching practice in case you're interested in a coaching session.
You can also read about workshops, classes and short talks on
creativity. On my website you can read some of my coaching
columns and articles from *Art Focus Oklahoma* magazine and
newspaper articles. Of course, there's a link to buy additional
copies of this book.

It's my hope that the stories and strategies in the pages of this
book and the on-line questions will inspire you to claim your
creative life and live it with joy.

God bless you! Stay in the process!
Romney Oualline Nesbitt

Printed in the United States
120886LV00001B/52-135/P